I saw a new heaven and a new earth . . .

Revelation 21:1

To David and Jayne Conner

Acknowledgements

I am enormously grateful to Joan Hart and Margaret Widdess for typing and reading the manuscript, and in Geneva to my colleagues and friends Freda Rajotte, Cécile de Sweemer, Gudrun Smith, Todor Sabev, Bernd Schulze, Uwe Arnhold, and Peter Tibbetts.

David Gosling

The author and publishers are also grateful to Alf Osmond for permission to incorporate his JPIC logo in the cover design and to Christian Aid for their generous contribution towards the cost of publication as a sign of their association with this book and with the issues it raises.

A NEW EARTH

Covenanting for Justice, Peace and the
Integrity of Creation

David Gosling

WITH THE COMPLIMENTS OF

DAVID GOSLING

CCBI
Inter-Church House
35 – 41 Lower Marsh
London SE1 7RL

David L. Gosling trained as a nuclear physicist before ordination and was director of Church and Society of the World Council of Churches from 1984 to 1989. He is currently Spalding Fellow in the University of Cambridge at Clare Hall.

ISBN 0 85169 222 2

Published by CCBI
Inter-Church House
35 – 41 Lower Marsh
London SE1 7RL

Cover design by Mark Whitchurch

Typeset and printed on recycled paper by
Delta Press, Brighton, East Sussex

Ref 219 KC

Contents

Foreword   *by the Archbishop of York* vii

Chapter 1   **Reassessing Nature's Place** 1
       (i)   Nature devalued. 1
       (ii)   Public awareness 2
       (iii)   Response of the churches 4

Chapter 2   **Creation under Threat** 9
       (i)   Creation's integrity 9
       (ii)   Africa 11
       (iii)   Latin America 13
       (iv)   Southeast Asia. 14
       (v)   The western world. 19
       (vi)   Theological and religious perspectives...... 22

Chapter 3   **Responding to Crises** 31
       (i)   Marshalls team visit. 31
       (ii)   Access to health 33
       (iii)   License to kill?. 37
       (iv)   Chernobyl 39
       (v)   World Environment Day 41
       (vi)   AIDS 43

Chapter 4   **Creation at the Centre** 49
       (i)   Work ethics. 51
       (ii)   Computers at the workplace. 54
       (iii)   Relating science and religion 56
       (iv)   Co-creators or co-workers? 60
       (v)   Cancelling the debts 62
       (vi)   Theocentric ethics. 64
       (vii)   Global consensus? 70

Chapter 5   **From Basle to Britain**. 73
       (i)   Basle's unique assembly. 73
       (ii)   A vision of Europe 76
       (iii)   Our Common Future. 81
       (iv)   Secular ethics. 84
       (v)   British JPIC initiatives 87
       (vi)   Enlarging the framework. 90

Chapter 6   **Agenda for the Nineties**. 93
       (i)   Design for living 96

       Appendix 103
       Select Bibliography 105
       Index of Names. 107

Foreword

One of the persistent weaknesses of the ecumenical movement has been loss of memory. This is particularly apparent at a time like the present when the generation of ecumenical pioneers who built the World Council of Churches has almost disappeared, and when today's problems are tackled by people with little or no knowledge of the work of their predecessors. In a cynical mood it sometimes seems as if every major world conference is doomed to start again from the beginning, with the result that it progresses no further, and sometimes less far, than those which preceded it.

Mature reflection on the work of ecumenical bodies must therefore play a vital part in the task of making them more effective. In one limited field this is what this book provides. It tells the story of how a single sub-unit in the World Council of Churches went about its task, tried – not always successfully – to develop some coherent lines of study and action, and sought to relate these to the remainder of the Council's work and to the pressing world problems which formed its agenda. On one level, therefore, it is a timely exercise in ecumenical self-examination.

On another level it provides a useful introduction to some of the themes which are central to today's environmental debate, brings Christian insight to bear on them, and relates them both to their local contexts and to global needs. The general work of the WCC in this field has been summed up since the 1983 Vancouver Assembly in the slogan 'Justice, Peace and the Integrity of Creation'. Some react to such slogans with enthusiasm, others with apathy and bewilderment. This book helps to unwrap some of its meaning, and can act as a useful study guide to those who have caught some of the vision behind the words and wonder what can be done about it. The fact that much of the work done by the sub-unit was based on local projects, carried out for the most part by local people, gives it roots in reality which high-flown generalisations about world issues frequently lack.

David Gosling was director of the sub-unit of Church and Society during most of the period about which he writes. As Moderator of its Working Committee I can vouch for the accuracy of the story he tells. Few people are better equipped to tell it. A university lecturer in both nuclear physics and theology with experience in many parts of the world, including India and Thailand, he has been particularly concerned about the impact of science and technology on developing countries and ancient cultures. There is a quiet passion for justice underneath this technical exposition of complex social and scientific problems. And behind the seemingly casual references to events in many parts of the world there lies a massive programme of world travel and personal contacts which give authority to his judgements.

It is a story well worth reading, and one which should encourage Christians who may be tempted to ask what, if anything, the Churches are trying to do about our spoilt earth. Its publication is particularly timely in view of the Earth Summit due to take place in Rio de Janeiro in June 1992.

John Habgood
Archbishop of York
April 1992

1 Reassessing Nature's Place

In 1983 representatives of three hundred mainly Protestant churches meeting in Vancouver decided to covenant for Justice, Peace and the Integrity of Creation. The third part of the phrase was new, and echoed what during the seventies had been the growing conviction of many churches that environmental problems must be taken at least as seriously as the ones more familiarly addressed under the headings of justice (e.g. human rights) or peace (e.g. nuclear disarmament). The 1991 Canberra Assembly endorsed the Vancouver call to the churches, emphasising the need to explore the connections between the elements of JPIC and its regional implications.

The Earth Summit in Rio de Janeiro in June 1992 under the auspices of the United Nations is indicative of the extent to which the environment is now a central political issue for every government. Among those represented at non-governmental level is the Council for Churches for Britain and Ireland (CCBI), whose brief contribution is included as an appendix. The reasoning underlying this statement, with its emphasis on the need to balance justice and 'green' issues against one another, has been largely shaped by JPIC thinking.

What brought environmental problems onto the agenda of the churches and how they have been tackled is a major concern of what follows. But first it will be helpful to consider why the environment has been treated with such disregard for so long and what has brought it into the centre of attention in Britain during the last few years. Later we shall explore the way the same issues have been experienced and responded to in other parts of the world.

(i) Nature devalued

It is sometimes claimed that Christianity or at least the Judaeo-Christian tradition is responsible for the lack of concern of the past few centuries for the state of the environment. This argument is not convincing, and illustrations will be given in later sections of the way the Bible and church tradition in different parts of the world affirm the value of creation in its totality.

As far as the recent past in Europe is concerned the denial of value to nature was particularly strong in the eighteenth century, and is reflected in the works of Immanuel Kant. Kant believed that nature is a collection of irrational forces to be subdued and kept in check by human effort. God is absolutely world-transcendent and nature is absolutely non-divine.

Thus, according to Kant, nature is the arena for humanity to achieve 'spiritual' freedom, irrespective of any moral limits on the means whereby this is achieved, or the possibility that nature may itself possess internal limits. Nature has no intrinsic value (i.e. value in itself), no part of it (e.g. animals) has any rights, and its worth is purely instrumental and subordinate to 'man'.

It is not surprising that when Kant and his followers read the Bible they emphasised the passages which seemed to uphold their world-view e.g. the exhortations to Adam in Genesis 1 to 'fill the earth and subdue it, rule over . . . every living thing'. Selective attention to certain parts of the Bible coupled with selective inattention to others (e.g. passages in the Psalms, Job and the Wisdom literature generally) would have seemed to endorse Kant's belittling view of non-human nature.

The nineteenth century added to Kant's clinical analysis of nature's subordinate role a psychological dimension which came to the fore in the furore which followed the publication of *Origin of Species* in 1859. The ensuing controversy is often represented as a confrontation between churchmen and scientists, and there were certainly some acrimonious debates between the two. But to the majority of people – then as probably now – such issues were largely peripheral, and it was only because they touched upon certain gut feelings that there was a dramatic upsurge in public interest.

Whatever the implications for Christian orthodoxy of Darwin's theory that higher animals and humans have evolved via struggle from lower forms of life, public opinion seemed to be shocked by the possibility that humans and animals have a common ancestry. This is reflected in cartoons in *Punch* and the rhetoric of public speakers such as the one who ended a speech with the appeal: 'Leave my ancestors in Paradise and I will allow you yours in the Zoological Gardens'. From these and similar examples and instances (e.g. the use of language to depreciate non-human life: 'brute' force, 'apeing' another person), we may infer that the attitude to nature set out by Kant had become deeply imprinted in the Victorian psyche, and was being challenged.

(ii) **Public awareness**

Why has nature now become so important and central in public debate, and slowly but increasingly, in the life of the churches?

During the 1960's attention was focussed on the environment from several directions: nuclear tests were seen to have global dimensions, lakes died, there was the *Torrey Canyon* oil spillage, road traffic went up and photochemical smog began to affect the middle classes, Rachel Carson's *Silent Spring* was published, and people saw the earth from space and sensed its vulnerability.

A decade later some of the worst predictions of energy shortages had not materialised, and the embryo environmental movement became stronger through a period of economic recession. Its hope for a rational use of the physical environment aroused wide interest among groups which included royalty and students. But increasingly, economic growth and environmental protection were seen by environmentalists as incompatible, and the subsequent polarisation in West Germany provoked Helmut Köhl into a disparaging comparison between environmentalists and tomatoes: 'they start green and finish up red'.

Much of the 1970's was preoccupied with energy rather than directly with the environment, but it is nonetheless surprising how little attention was paid to environmental problems in *North-South*, the Report of an Independent Commission on International Development Issues, chaired by Willy Brandt, published in 1980. The eleven-page summary of its recommendations includes only the following short paragraph pertaining directly to the environment:

> The strain on the global environment derives mainly from the growth of the industrial economies, but also from that of the world's population. It threatens the survival and development opportunities of future generations. All nations have to cooperate more urgently in international management of the atmosphere and other global commons, and in the prevention of irreversible ecological damage.[1]

In spite of the lack of priority given by the *Brandt Report* to specifically environmental issues, there was considerable interest in the UK in its proposals for reforming the international economy. The churches played a major part in a lobby of Parliament organised by the World Development Movement in 1981.

In essence the Brandt proposals attempted to redress the problems of the global North-South divide with rational arguments appealing to everybody's self-interest. Industrial countries would benefit from stable oil prices, oil producers would have access to markets and technology, poor countries would receive additional aid and newly industrialised countries would benefit from a reduction in tariffs enabling them to sell their goods. But there was no discussion of the conditions for giving and repaying aid, economic and political conflict between the four groups of nations just mentioned, or the assumptions underlying international economic relationships.

During the second half of the 1970's many developing countries borrowed in dollars from the commercial banks in order to finance

---

1 *North-South: A Programme for Survival*, Pan Books, 1980, p. 283.

imports, the cost of which had rocketed as a result of sharp oil price increases. Dollar values went up, rates of interest in the United States rose – which meant that commercial banks lent at higher rates of interest, and the value of exports produced in developing countries (their main source of repaying debts) declined. These and other factors plunged many developing countries into debt.

The debts of developing countries are now recognised to have considerable implications for the state of the environment and possibilities for improvement. Public awareness, however, scarcely moved beyond the superficial concern of the late sixties. Energy became the centre of public attention in the seventies, and although the *Brandt Report* was the focus of a huge public lobby of Parliament, it never addressed the structural problems which are the root cause of much environmental damage and which must be resolved before significant improvement can occur. Insofar as these problems are essentially to do with justice, it will be apparent that any analysis which begins by addressing the state of the environment quickly moves into areas more familiar under the headings of 'justice', and, as will become clearer presently, of 'peace'. This is one of the interpretations intended by the Vancouver delegates in calling the churches to covenant for Justice, Peace and the Integrity of Creation.

(iii) Response of the churches

The sixties and seventies saw little organised response to environmental problems on the part of the churches, though quite a number of church members may have belonged to organisations such as Friends of the Earth, Greenpeace and the various animal rights groups.

In 1970 the Church of Scotland set up its Society, Religion and Technology (SRT) Project, and several important environmental issues were subsequently addressed. These included a study of the effects of oil on social structures, the distribution of wealth, the assimilation of workers from outside Scotland and the environmental impact of the oil industry as a whole. In 1975 a study was made of the effects of agricultural chemical networks on the Third World. Scotland's traditional closeness between 'Church' and 'society' made it possible for SRT staff to draw upon the best expertise available and readily disseminate their findings.

Insofar as energy policy has major environmental implications, the British Council of Churches' public hearing in 1976 on the feasibility of building a commercial fast reactor was a significant event.[2] Ten of the thirty-three expert witnesses who gave evidence represented

2 Hugh Montefiore and David Gosling, eds., *Nuclear Crisis: A Question of Breeding*, Prism Press, 1977.

environmentally-related organisations, and the panel which cross-examined them included key figures from the fuel industries.

The findings of this public hearing, which was arranged in response to a request by the then Secretary of State for Energy, Tony Benn (who gave evidence), were used by the BCC to present a case at the Windscale Public Local Inquiry the following summer. The essence of the BCC's case was that a convergence of social and environmental factors argued against the building of a nuclear reprocessing plant until various conditions and criticisms had been met. These were: a reduction in the level of disagreement among experts relating to relevant technical issues, the need for a satisfactory commercial solution to the safe long-term disposal of reprocessing wastes, the prospect of unacceptable limitations on civil liberties and increased risks of proliferation caused by the increased use of plutonium, the foreclosing of alternative energy options, the relative insignificance of arguments for the proposal based on foreign earnings and employment opportunities, and the objection to embarking upon a development which significantly increases the burden of responsibility, and potentially, of risk, to our descendants.

Thus although the focus of the Windscale Inquiry was future energy options, much of the debate was about environmental risks. The BCC's case was not anti-nuclear *per se,* but the confrontational format of the Inquiry and the abrasive disposition of its Inspector, Lord Parker, made it virtually impossible to distinguish between the blanket opposition to nuclear power of, say, Friends of the Earth, and the BCC's conditional affirmation of it. The BCC's call for a hierarchy of moral presumptions derived from a tradition based on Christian and Humanist elements was regarded with interest, and the proposal for a nuclear ombudsman was taken up in the Inquiry Report.[3]

Shortly afterwards, the Church of Scotland's SRT Project started an energy conservation programme which included studies of energy efficiency and the environmental impact of different energy sources. This was in line with the Government's energy efficiency programme and was partly funded by Government. In view of Scotland's investment in oil and military nuclear installations, it is not surprising that the SRT studies concentrated on oil and the nuclear option, though attention was also paid to the renewables (wind, wave and solar) and their environmental impact (by no means negligible).

The Home Mission Division of the Methodist Church published two highly competent, though very different, reports, *Shaping Tomorrow* and

3 For details of the case presented see David Gosling, 'The Morality of Nuclear Power' in *Theology,* Vol. LXXXI, No. 679, January 1978, p. 25.

Future Conditional, in 1981 and 1983 respectively.[4] The former addressed important specific issues such as the treatment of battery hens, but the latter tackled more fundamental questions about limits to human behaviour in relation to non-human life and the ecosystem, and gave a useful definition of sustainability – which in the seventies had become a catch-all word for just about everything – in terms of ecological economics:

> The question of *sustainability* is the question of ecological economics, of the relationship between human and non-human life forms. In the Bible, these and inanimate creation, too, are linked together in the phrase 'all God's works'. Animals, plants and human life, the earth and the heavens, are all God's creation. Within this creation, humanity has a special role: on the one hand, 'to rule the fish in the sea, the birds of heaven, the cattle, all wild animals on earth, and all reptiles that crawl upon the earth' (Gen. 1:26); but on the other hand, not to do so without limitation: 'You may eat from every tree in the garden, but not from the tree of knowledge of good and evil' (Gen. 2:17). To put the same point differently, human domination of the non-human world is part of our sharing in the 'image of God' (Gen. 1:27): our dominion over created things has to be exercised in the same way that God exercised domination, with care and love . . . Similarly, too, are we bound together with the rest of creation in our need for, and the possibility of, redemption (Is. 10:33–11:9; 65:25).[5]

The response of the World Council of Churches to environmental issues prior to the 1983 Vancouver Assembly lagged behind that of some of the churches mentioned (e.g. in Scotland). The notion of the Just, Participatory and Sustainable Society (JPSS) dominated WCC thinking between the 1975 Nairobi Assembly and Vancouver, and was not conducive to serious reflection about the non-human world.

The WCC's ability to respond was also limited by its division into small sub-units positioned in larger units in such a manner that programme staff with shared concerns had difficulty working together. In the autumn of 1991 the entire WCC was restructured, and several of the sub-units to which reference will be made in this and subsequent chapters were combined under the common head 'Justice, Peace, Creation' – an indication of how seriously the WCC continues to regard the whole JPIC process. We shall therefore not consider the earlier small sub-units in any

4 *Shaping Tomorrow,* Home Mission Division of the Methodist Church, 1981; *Future Conditional,* Home Mission Division of the Methodist Church, 1983.
5 *Future Conditional,* p. 7.

detail. Our main concern will be with Church and Society, which, until its recent demise, was essentially the WCC's 'think tank'.

Prior to the Vancouver Assembly Church and Society adopted very much a 'top down' approach to issues which appealed primarily to North Atlantic liberals in search of global alternatives to capitalism and communism. Science and technology featured extensively in its programme from about 1970 onwards, and discussions about energy and the finiteness of fuel resources took precedence over concern about ecology and the state of the environment, though a consultation held at the Ecumenical Institute at Bossey in 1978 singled out justice and ecology as 'the twin issues around which the world's future revolves'. But this consultation, which raised renewable 'alternatives' to the level of fully-fledged energy sources, was exceptional in that it included representatives from European and US environmental groups, including Chris Cowap, director of Church and Society for the US National Council of Churches, who did pioneering work among 'grass-root' women's groups prior to her untimely death from cancer.

For the most part the attitude to the environment of the Church and Society constituency during the 1970's was one of pragmatic instrumentalism, and Vancouver's rejection of sustainability in the JPSS in favour of integrity of creation in JPIC was greeted with dismay. But by then the churches in both halves of Germany and parts of Scandinavia and Canada had become heavily involved in environmental issues, and representatives of Pacific churches, some of whom had experienced first hand the effects of the 1950's nuclear bomb tests, were all set to shock the Vancouver delegates into a re-evaluation of the entire ecumenical agenda.

2 Creation under Threat

Christians believe that God works in and through the created universe and is drawing it into a single, integrated whole. This process is uneven and often seems arbitrary, with the result that both those who try to be in tune with it and those who do not receive knocks and collide with forces not of their own or even human making.

The wholeness towards which God's creative spirit draws the universe is not achievable in this life. It is located in the future, where the biblical word for peace, *shalom*, best describes its character, and in the life of Jesus Christ, who is the sign of that future hope. Christians believe that Jesus was supremely open to the creative spirit of God, colliding with but ultimately overcoming the dark forces of injustice and evil in the world.

The duty of the Church is to be a sign of the world's coming into being, inviting people to participate in God's creative activity, which encompasses the whole of creation. God's future kingdom of peace is being realised in many ways by many different types of people; what makes the Church distinctive in this respect is not that it does this better, but that it can *interpret* what is happening. The Church is called by God to articulate the vision of *shalom* (Christ ascended), our yearning and the yearning of the whole of creation for it, and to define the path to be taken in terms of what we can see in the life and teaching of Jesus Christ – a path that is celebrated in worship whereby Christians offer the world to God and pray that it may achieve its destiny.

Thus we understand 'creation', which is fundamental, 'peace', which defines creation's destiny, and 'justice', which expresses the steady pressure of God's spirit and our own efforts towards wholeness, community and interdependence.

(i) Creation's integrity

We saw in chapter one that nature came to be devalued but that we are now being obliged to reconsider our relationship with the world around us. The phrase 'integrity of creation' which emerged at the 1983 Vancouver Assembly is a challenge to the churches to rediscover a sense of the wholeness and interrelatedness of creation and the need for appropriate action to renew and nourish it. We must therefore examine this curious phrase, which the German delegates at Vancouver declared untranslatable, and delegates to the 1989 Basle Assembly of European churches avoided altogether.

Integrity – implying uprightness and honesty in people, and wholeness, soundness, entirety more generally – is a relational word. Theologically, in relation to God, 'integrity of creation' implies both the dependence of creation on its Creator and the worth and dignity of creation in its own right (i.e. its intrinsic value). The phrase therefore invites us to reaffirm the fundamental Christian truth that all that exists, seen and unseen, has God as its author.

Horizontally, the integrity of creation implies that every creature is bound to every other creature in a community and communion of being. Human beings especially must recognise that we are not separate from and above the rest of creation, but part of its totality, sharing with other living beings their limitations and destiny. Though separated from direct contact with the source of our livelihood by agriculture and industry, we none the less receive our life and food daily from our Creator.

We saw in the last section that 'wholeness' (i.e. integrity), though not achievable in this life, is an essential characteristic of *shalom*, the future goal towards which God's creative spirit and our own efforts draw the entire creation. Integrity of creation captures the dynamism of that vision and the inclusiveness which we have only very recently begun to take seriously. And just as a person of integrity is recognised as one who both is, descriptively, integrated ('has got their act together'), and also acts in certain kinds of ways, so the integrity of creation suggests that wholesome relationships between God, humanity and nature will produce action for justice and peace.

Although peace in the ultimate sense of *shalom* is not attainable in this life, we act as 'peace makers' – that special category of people who are unconditionally blessed in the Sermon on the Mount – whenever we heal divisions. In the Old Testament peace is the state of a healthy society, where the dignity, worth and rights of every individual are cherished. Peace is incompatible with physical violence, of course, but the Old Testament prophets knew very well that violence is often built into the social, economic and political structures of society (e.g. Jeremiah 6: 14). In the New Testament the supreme act of peace is Jesus Christ's breaking down of the wall of hostility between Jews and Gentiles (Ephesians 2: 14). A powerful contemporary illustration of peace is the collapse of the Berlin Wall.

Just as many people think of peace as the mere absence of violence without regard to deeper structural dislocations, so justice is often equally superficially understood as 'fairness' or 'sharing with others'. But justice in the Old Testament is rooted in the will of God, which displays such a consistent bias in favour of the poor and oppressed that it may appear unfair! Some of Jesus' parables are almost perverse in the way they reverse conventional notions of justice e.g. the story of the labourers who receive the same pay for one hour's work as the ones who worked all day (Matthew 20: 1–16). The modern ecumenical movement lays great store by the need to confront unjust social, economic and political structures which many people never question, but which are the cause of enormous human suffering. A powerful contemporary illustration of justice is the movement which secured Nelson Mandela's release from prison.

'Covenanting' for Justice, Peace and the Integrity of Creation is often taken to mean little more than 'commitment' to JPIC issues. But it is much stronger than that. In day-to-day usage a covenant is a binding agreement between two or more roughly equal parties – thus churchgoers may covenant sums of money to the weekly church collection. In biblical usage one of the covenanting parties is usually God, who promises us certain things in return for faithfulness. At the conclusion of the Flood God made a covenant with Noah that it would not happen again, and the rainbow became the sign of that enduring promise (Genesis 9: 16).

Some churches attribute more importance to covenanting than others. The Reformed Churches, for example, understand both Old and New Testaments as a sequence of covenants established by God with all people. In Britain a more evocative example of a covenant is the bonding of Dresden and Coventry after the last War. Such a covenant for peace, sealed by the silent witness of two ruined and resurrected cathedrals, speaks much more eloquently than any number of conference resolutions. It is also acceptable to all shades of theological and political opinion and hence potentially 'conciliar' – a word widely canvassed in ecumenical circles to express the hope of a consensus.

We shall return to the theological aspects of JPIC later. In the next section we shall explore the way concern for the environment emerged in different parts of the world from the early 1980's onwards, and how churches and other bodies responded.

(ii) Africa

In August 1981 the WCC presented a case for the stewardship of energy at the UN Conference on New and Renewable Energy Sources in Nairobi. In keeping with the high level of concern at that time about escalating oil prices and the need to find alternatives to diminishing conventional fuel supplies, several heads of State participated, including Indira Gandhi and Pierre Trudeau. Britain was represented by a junior minister and the Vatican's seat remained vacant throughout.

Details of the conference and the WCC's case, which was couched in terms of the pre-Vancouver Just, Participatory and Sustainable Society (JPSS) need not trouble us here. What was remarkable was the huge demonstrations organised by local environmental organisations, including the Kenyan churches.

The main concern of the tens of thousands of demonstrators was deforestation. It was also clear that it was the poorer sections of local communities, both rural and urban, which were the hardest hit, and among them especially women, who were being obliged to walk further and further to find firewood. The shiny photovoltaic cells and other renewable energy devices displayed by the UN Environment Programme and other bodies were far too expensive for them, and there was no evidence of a viable market mechanism to bring prices to within their reach.

This particular conference illustrates very well the mood prevailing in the early 1980's. Governments, the UN, and the planners, were all preoccupied with global solutions to problems of fuel shortages expected before the end of the decade. But in reality the poorest sections of rural and urban communities were already suffering from the environmental side-effects of bad development promoted in some cases by the same bodies talking around the conference table about the need for a sustainable global future. From the point of view of our understanding of JPIC we therefore note that environmental degradation and the unjust suffering of particular vulnerable groups went hand in hand.

Visits to Africa and contributions by Africans to WCC consultations during the past few years indicate that there are a number of major different types of environmental problem. In Ghana and Burkina Faso, for example, the southward movement of the Sahara by approximately 15 kilometres a year is a major cause for concern which has led to the planting of huge reserves of eucalyptus trees which retain moisture at high temperatures. Nigeria is currently concerned about the illegal dumping of industrial waste, in some cases radioactive, on her coastline. A Namibian participant at an early JPIC consultation remarked on the irony of the situation whereby South African security forces defoliate land alongside roads used for transporting Namibian uranium which is then processed in South Africa to produce fissile material potentially usable in nuclear weapons designed to buttress the apartheid State. What more compelling evidence was needed, he argued, of the links between injustice, threats to peace and damage to the environment?

At the beginning of the 1990's Africa's economic and environmental problems remain vast and intractable. But there have been some gains, of which the introduction of agroforestry – the simultaneous growing of trees and crops – is possibly the most important. According to Paul Harrison:

Agroforesty is not only the most promising approach to reafforestation and the supply of fuel, it is also, in yield-boosting forms like windbreaks and alley-cropping, the most hopeful avenue for intensifying African agriculture over the next five to ten years, increasing food production and reducing exposure to drought with few or no outside or imported inputs.

Agroforestry is arguably the single most important discipline for the future of sustainable development in Africa.[6]

More will be said about sustainable development in chapter five. We now consider other geographical regions.

(iii) Latin America

Welcoming delegates to the WCC Central Committee in Buenos Aires in 1985 the then President of Argentina, Raoul Alfonsin, gave a graphic account of the effects of environmental degradation on various parts of South America and the reasons why these are aggravated by crippling debts to the international banks. In an attempt to repay loans used in many cases to service unsatisfactory development programmes, governments were being forced to 'buy' foreign currency (the only acceptable form of repayment) by growing cash crops for export. These were best grown on plantations created by the destruction of forests the original inhabitants of which were then obliged to move further and further away or seek poorly paid employment in mushrooming congested cities or as plantation workers.

Fertilisers were introduced to increase crop yields and pesticides were then needed to control the accompanying pests. Native Indians who had once lived self-sufficiently on the land became poorer and poorer. In some cases workers on plantations growing sugar, coffee and corn for export to rich nations were starving. And the governments best able to implement such harsh policies were inevitably military dictatorships which relished border skirmishes with their neighbours, purchasing their armaments with the same hard-earned foreign exchange more urgently needed to pay off their national debts.

President Alfonsin's solution to these problems was to cancel the debts and start all over again. The churches and the WCC should call for a debt jubilee corresponding to the Jewish practice of emancipating people and land every fifty years. Unless this happened, he argued, we would all suffer irretrievably.

This analysis illustrates very clearly from the perspective of Latin America how JPIC issues are intertwined, and the consequent impos-

6 Paul Harrison, *The Greening of Africa*, Paladin, 1987, p. 204.

sibility, for example, of solving Brazil's deforestation problems without reference to the unjust exploitation of people and the military ambitions of successive governments. The debt problem, which began as a flow of resources from developed to developing nations, has now become a reverse flow from the Third World to the First. Christian Aid estimates that this is equivalent every year to each man, woman and child in the developing world paying £2.50 to the industrial nations – which is many times more than could ever be raised by the churches of developed countries to help the poor!

Brazil's natural resources, which include 40% of the world's tropical forests and one-third of its living species, play a vital role in regulating our global ecosystem. Recent discoveries about the greenhouse effect and ozone layer depletion make it imperative that new strategies are quickly found to preserve our planetary 'lungs' – the forests of the Amazon in particular – from complete breakdown.

Tropical rain forests are currently disappearing at the rate of one football field every second. There are approximately two million less Amazonian trees per day to absorb atmospheric carbon dioxide, which we now know to be building up at an alarming rate. This is causing increases in global average temperatures and consequent melting of glaciers and expansion of water leading to sea level rises possibly in excess of a metre by mid-next century. No amount of reafforestation, as in the sub-Sahara, can replace the estimated million varieties of species which will have disappeared forever by the year 2000 if present trends continue.

Two consultations held in São Paulo, Brazil, and San José, Costa Rica, in mid-1988, explored these and associated problems such as industrial and urban air and water pollution. Visits were made to Cubatão, currently the world's most polluted city, on the Brazilian coast near São Paulo, where a Roman Catholic priest registers his protest by reading out during Sunday Mass the death certificates of all those whose deaths can be attributed to pollution. Most at risk are Brazil's thirty-five million children who live below the poverty line and whose sufferings were vividly portrayed several years ago in the widely-circulated film 'Pixote'. During our visit to São Paulo the star actor in this powerful film, then a boy of eleven, was murdered by the police.

(iv) **Southeast Asia**

A WCC consultation held in Manila in 1986 on 'New Technology, Work and the Environment' (see Table I) studied a wide range of environmental issues which included the Bhopal disaster, nuclear testing in the Marshall Islands and the attempted destruction of the Greenpeace ship *Rainbow Warrior*, in Auckland Harbour. Manila is situated approximately at the centre of a triangle marking these three events.

Table I: Conferences mentioned in the text

Date	Place	Title	Sponsored by
1981 August	Nairobi	New and Renewable Energy	United Nations
1983 June	Amsterdam	Science Education and Ethics	Free University in Amsterdam, WCC Church and Society
July	Vancouver	Jesus Christ, the Life of the World	WCC Assembly
1984 September	Glasgow	Technology, Employment and Rapid Social Change	Church of Scotland SRT Project, WCC Church and Society
1985 July	Buenos Aires	Central Committee	WCC Central Committee
1986 January	Manila	New Technology, Work and the Environment	NCC Philippines, WCC Church and Society
March	Geneva	JPIC Preparatory Meeting	WCC JPIC
May	York	Integrity of Creation	WCC Faith and Order and Church and Society
June	Cartigny, Switzerland	AIDS and the Church	WCC Church and Society, Christian Medical Commission, Education
July	Potsdam, GDR	Working Committee	WCC Church and Society
October	Salatiga, Indonesia	Science Education	Free University in Amsterdam, WCC Church and Society
November	Glion, Switzerland	JPIC Preparatory Meeting	WCC JPIC
1987 January	Geneva	Central Committee	WCC Central Committee
May	Amsterdam	Reintegrating God's Creation	WCC Church and Society
September	Glion, Switzerland	Working Committee	WCC Church and Society
October	Marshall Islands	Team Visit	WCC Church and Society, Christian Medical Commission
1988 February	Granvöllen, Norway	JPIC Preparatory Meeting	WCC JPIC
April	Bossey, Switzerland	Science and the Theology of Creation	WCC Ecumenical Institute, Church and Society
May	Dublin	Creation and the Kingdom of God	WCC Faith and Order, Church and Society
June	São Paulo	God, People and Nature	WCC Church and Society
July	San José	Tropical Forest Conservation	WCC Church and Society
August	Hanover	Central Committee	WCC Central Committee
September	Annecy	Theocentric Ethics	WCC Church and Society
September	Tambov, USSR	Working Committee	WCC Church and Society
1989 May	Basle	Peace with Justice	European Assembly
November	Sofia	Working Committee	WCC Church and Society
1990 March	Seoul	JPIC World Congress	WCC JPIC
1991 February	Canberra	Come Holy Spirit: Renew the Whole Creation	WCC Assembly
1992 June	Rio de Janeiro	Earth Summit	United Nations

The consultation took place shortly before the end of the Marcos régime, and the two main opening speakers, Cardinal Sin and Methodist Bishop La Verne Mercado, lost no opportunity in condemning government excesses. One participant, Fidel Nemenzo, a young mathematician from the University of the Philippines, had been shot and almost killed during a peaceful demonstration shortly before our meeting. One of the organisers from Geneva was soaked with water cannon during an equally peaceful march to commemorate Human Rights Day. As the Military prepared to use tear gas, a Roman Catholic nun produced a gauze face mask and a small *lemoncito* fruit to squeeze around the edges: 'Appropriate technology', she explained.

The Bhopal disaster and problems of radiation-exposed Marshall Islanders will be described in the next chapter. Nearer home to the predominantly Southeast Asian conference participants were the issues of deforestation and marine pollution, damaging side effects (e.g. eye deterioration) from the manufacture and use of computers, and the consequences of wide-scale use of monosodium glutamate (MSG) as a food additive. A Japanese professor also gave some grim examples of mercury poisoning arising from Japan's chemical industry, and two professors from Indonesia and the Philippines argued fiercely over the merits and demerits of nuclear power in the region.

Much of what has been said about Africa and Latin America applies also to Southeast Asia, and the links between environmental, justice and peace issues were felt to be very strong – possibly more so in the Philippines than anywhere else. British ecologist Norman Myers claimed that deforestation is proceeding more rapidly in Southeast Asia than anywhere else in the world. If present land-use patterns continue, soon none of the most valuable forests will be left except in Papua New Guinea, and the entire forest resource may have disappeared in most parts of the Philippines, Malaysia, Indonesia, Burma and Thailand.[7]

Myers' analysis considered the relative effects of commercial logging and damage by small-scale cultivators, concluding that the former are more readily able to adapt their practices to make them benign to forest environments. This option is seldom open to landless peasants, many of whom have been forced off their land to make way for plantations to grow cash crops for export – as in the case of Brazil. Myers also believes that although population increases put pressure on forest ecosystems, much more damage is done by commercial loggers and displaced landless peasants.

7 Norman Myers, 'Deforestation and Development in Asia', in Feliciano Carino and David Gosling, eds., *Technology from the Underside*, NCCP, 1986, p. 17.

The plight of women workers in the microelectronics industry was a major cause for concern. In many parts of Southeast Asia multinationals employ large numbers of young women to produce circuits for microchips. The technology looks clean and sophisticated, but pay is very poor, and the workers' eyesight may be permanently damaged as a result of long hours peering through microscopes. Wazir-Jahan Karim, a Malaysian journalist, gave a graphic account of the exploitation of young, single, rural migrant women, aged between about 18 and 24 years.

> These women enjoy a peculiarly ambivalent status in the traditional rural communities. Though subject to strong parental and family discipline, they are at the same time relatively free to pursue further education and employment, and very often develop a strong sense of independence and freedom from village traditions when they join the production line. However, from a management point of view, in the factories they are docile and easily manageable, and indeed, these supposed characteristics of theirs are used unashamedly as attractions for foreign investors. The ability of these women to sit for hours carrying out a tedious, repetitive task is apparently a major reason why foreign companies invest in Malaysia.[8]

By contrast, the same multinationals operating in Northern Europe, Scotland, for example, employ a small labour force, with the result that the same population groups which in Southeast Asia are underpaid and overworked, are predominantly unemployed – the young, and especially women.[9]

The nuclear power debate at the Manila consultation was primarily about fuel resources rather than the environment as such, but it illustrated some of the links between peace and justice issues, which can on occasion operate in opposite directions.

From the point of view of most Southeast Asian states arguments for nuclear power based on projected fuel shortages are not convincing. Thailand, for example, possesses substantial quantities of natural gas and a relatively small population (55 million) in quite a large and predominantly rural area. Nuclear power is therefore not needed. The same is true for the Philippines.

Indonesia's situation is entirely different. With a population of almost 180 million increasing at a rate of 2.3% per annum, Indonesia is currently

8 Wazir-Jahan Karim, 'Electronic Woman', In Carino and Gosling, *Ibid.*, p. 26.
9 Howard Davis and David Gosling, eds., *Will the Future Work?*, WCC, Geneva, 1986.

geared to a period of rapid industrialisation which will quickly exhaust most non-renewable conventional fuel supplies – oil, coal and natural gas. There is a small potential for geothermal and hydro-electric power and some non-nuclear renewables such as wind, solar energy and biogas could be used in rural areas. But Java's population of 90 million packed into fifty thousand square miles cannot afford the space for most renewables, and Indonesian coal, though still plentiful, contains high proportions of sulphur and sodium, which cause severe health problems in such densely populated areas.

The argument for nuclear power in Indonesia was strongly advocated at the Manila and Salatiga consultations by Liek Wilardjo, a nuclear scientist at Satya Wacana Christian University, who delivered an impassioned plea to delegates to understand why there is no alternative to nuclear power in Indonesia, and not to apply double standards by refusing to support in developing countries types of technology which had assisted the First World to industrialise:

> We are aware of the not-too-effectiveness of the International Atomic Energy Authority as the international safeguard against nuclear arms proliferation. Yet as a good citizen of the World Community, Indonesia has been willing to play along with the rules-signing and ratifying the Nuclear Non-Proliferation Treaty (NPT), for example. We only hope that the six members of the Nuclear Club, and those countries with advanced nuclear technology which could readily join it if and when they so wish, will . . . refrain from applying a double standard: one (the very lenient one) for themselves, and the other (the one with too many and too strict restrictions) for the non-nuclear, developing countries. Ignore this appeal, and do not be surprised to learn that the developing countries will soon lose their faith in the theme 'Justice, Participation and Sustainability'.

Such arguments are deeply felt in many developing countries. Safeguard peace by limiting the spread of nuclear technology, and you act unjustly. Behave justly by enabling every country that wants nuclear technology to have it, and you threaten peace. Yet neither argument addresses the fundamental problems of structural injustice underlying all relationships between developed and developing countries.

In spite of evidence presented in many papers at the Manila consultation of damage caused by science and technology, the final report was optimistic about their overall potential value. Delegates urged the churches and their agencies 'to become active participants in the transformation both of technology and of the socio-economic and political context in which it operates'. Recommendations included the fostering of appropriate tree planting and agroforestry projects, the bringing together of decision-makers and individuals in positions of public responsibility into direct contact with people adversely affected by their decisions, practical assistance to vulnerable groups such as women in certain industries, the establishment of an information and action network to counter militarisation and related aspects of the development of nuclear power along the Pacific rim, and the replacement of the 'competitive and divisive' Protestant Work Ethic by 'a world-wide work ethic which both reflects regional religious and cultural traditions, and is sensitive both to short and long-term local and global environmental constraints'. This final recommendation picked up Cardinal Sin's opening call for an environmentally-sensitive work ethic. We shall say more about this in chapter four.

The problem of food additives such as MSG may be distinctive to Southeast Asia in that this particular 'appetiser' has been familiar for many centuries in small quantities in Chinese cooking. In larger quantities, however, it can cause cancer and brain damage, and the Japanese firm of Ajinomoto is currently involved in a massive drive to promote its use throughout the region. We shall see in chapter five how such a situation has been aggravated by short-sighted agricultural policies in Europe. The Manila delegates stressed the importance of making visible the economic and political structures which create and sustain such situations and the need to counter inaccurate and misleading advertising about certain foodstuffs, food additives and medicines by disseminating accurate information via women's groups, clergy, Buddhist monks and videos.[10]

Here, as in Latin America, the use of appropriate technology to counter misinformation and assist people's groups in their struggles against injustice was strongly encouraged. 'Appropriate' in such contexts does not mean 'simplistic' or 'unsophisticated'. In Argentina, for example, at the time of our visit, the Madres de la Plaza de Mayo, mothers of young men and women who 'disappeared' under successive repressive régimes, had devised a genetic data bank to provide proof of identity of their loved ones.

(v) The western world

We saw in the last chapter how concern in Britain about the state of the environment grew during the late 1960's, and, after a period of several years in the seventies during which everybody's attention was directed to fuel resources and oil price increases, has become a significant political

10 David Gosling, 'Thailand's Bare-headed Doctors', in *Modern Asian Studies*, Vol. 19, No. 4, Cambridge University Press 1984, p. 761.

issue in the 1992 General Election. But in spite of current interest in all things green, Britain has been *much* slower than most of Europe to come to terms with the environmental crises.

In both halves of united Germany there was a high level of environmental concern throughout the eighties, and East German peace groups were among the first to make connections between peace, justice and the environment. In West Germany the Protestant Church Convention (Kirchentag) has provided vast numbers of young Germans with an opportunity to channel their feelings along similar lines. Shortly before the Düsseldorf Kirchentag in June 1985 the Council of the Evangelical Church in Germany and the German Catholic Bishops' Conference issued a joint statement on ecological problems entitled 'Exercising Responsibility for the Creation'. This statement, the first of its kind, called for a fundamental change of attitude over our treatment of animals, plants and the world around us. Lifestyles and patterns of consumption must change, and economic theories must be brought into line with ecological principles. This would lead to 'a social market economy committed to environmental protection' together with 'full employment, monetary stability, a balance of foreign trade, a reasonable rate of economic growth and a just distribution of income'.[11]

By comparison with Germany the French have remained largely indifferent to environmental problems. Their refusal to end underground nuclear testing in French Polynesia and government complicity in the attack upon *Rainbow Warrior* have not endeared them to environmentalists, though sections of the Protestant churches have campaigned vigorously to end nuclear testing in the Pacific.

There has been little noticeable environmental activity in Spain and Italy, though the states bordering the Mediterranean have collectively made considerable progress in reducing marine pollution. Swiss environmental groups have been more active in the German-speaking part of the country, and it will be interesting to see how long it takes for administrators in Geneva to acknowledge the full extent of water-borne and air pollution in and around their beautiful mountain-fringed lake. The Chernobyl disaster, which thrust a giant plume of radioactivity south into Italy where northerly winds carried it to Zürich, was a salutary reminder to the Swiss that pollution is no respecter of national frontiers.

Before moving on from Switzerland it is important to note the part played in raising public awareness of environmental issues by the small UN Environment Programme (UNEP) office in Geneva. The headquarters of the UNEP are in Nairobi – an imaginative example of

11 'Joint Church Statement on Ecology' in the *EKD Bulletin*, No. 2, June 1985, p. 7.

decentralisation which might be imitated by other Geneva-based organisations, including the WCC – but the Geneva office has been active in promoting a variety of environmental activities such as a multi-faith celebration of World Environment Day in June 1986 at the WCC.

Scandinavian concern about the environment has been similar to that of Germany. Demonstrations against Mrs Thatcher's visit to Oslo showed the strength of Norwegian feeling about Britain's acid rain. Large parts of Scandinavia bore the brunt of the Chernobyl emissions with tragic consequences for their reindeer. Norway's already green image received a further boost with the appointment of Mrs Gro Harlem Brundtland as moderator of the UN Commission on Environment and Development which produced *Our Common Future.*

The former USSR appears for a long time to have regarded pollution as an unavoidable consequence of industrialisation. But the combination of Chernobyl and the new mood of openness signalled by Perestroika seems to have changed much of that. Although the Russians were criticised for their delay in admitting the full extent of the Chernobyl radioactive releases, their hesitation was not as reprehensible as Britain's concealment of the effects of the 1957 Windscale accident for more than thirty years. But in other parts of Eastern Europe some very ugly environmental sores have emerged: in Romania, for example.

Further afield, in the USA and Canada, lively and well-informed environmental organisations and groups have kept their governments on their toes. There, as elsewhere, the focus of the seventies was fuel supplies and oil prices, and it was impressive to see how President Carter's 1979 call for a fifty mile per hour speed limit to reduce petrol consumption was heeded by US citizens. Perhaps such responsible restraint could happen again in the USA along a wider range of environmental issues!

Chris Cowap's pioneering work with women's environmental groups in the USA has already been mentioned. Similar networking has occurred in Canada, where young Canadians have been quick to protest at the destruction of their lakes by acid rain from the US, and also to support claims by native Indians for land rights. In August 1986 the United Church of Canada's General Council passed a series of resolutions aimed at supporting small-scale farmers and fisherfolk, and challenging the 'bigger is better' mentality of government and business on the grounds that it had led to wastage, soil and plant deterioration and unemployment.[12]

In Australia uranium mining and the related problem of aboriginal land rights exercised environmentalists in the 1970s, but there has recently been a shift in public perception towards issues such as the phasing out

12 *Mandate,* Vol. 18, No. 4, United Church of Canada, 1987, p. 11.

of chlorofluorocarbons, which may partially reflect worries about Australia's proximity to areas directly beneath the Antarctic's ozone holes. Sewage disposal and the dumping of industrial waste in drains or in the sea have become major political issues in the last few years.

The environmental movement in the western world has not been without its internal divisions, especially those relating to the extent to which environmentalists try to work 'within the system' or adopt a more radical approach to the relationship between economics and ecology.[13]

The state of the environment has been a source of concern in many parts of the world which have not been mentioned – China, for example, where national days of tree planting have been introduced. What we have tried to demonstrate in this chapter is the variety of ways in which different countries are experiencing environmental problems – differences which call for a range of responses which take into account varying cultural, and, for the churches, theological traditions.

Underlying the differences, however, certain patterns emerge, of which the most significant for this study are the links between damage done to the environment and injustice to some or other vulnerable human group. Sometimes there have been violations of peace as well.

In the next section we shall consider some of the traditions from within which churches are beginning to respond. Once again no attempt will be made to present a comprehensive picture; it is the diversity that is significant.

(vi) **Theological and religious perspectives**

The theological introduction to this chapter is inclusive in the sense that when it comes to actually bringing *shalom* into being, as much significance is given to what may happen outside the Church as within it. The Church does not possess a monopoly of goodness or right action!

But we made one important qualification, namely that the Church, by virtue of its familiarity with the life of Christ, is able to *interpret* what is happening in the world. Its calling is to be a sign of the world's coming into being, channelling the yearning of all people and of the entire creation towards the overcoming of everything that is opposed to justice, peace and the integrity of God's creation. Whatever one may think of the WCC as an organisation, the Vancouver and Canberra affirmations of JPIC remain an important Christian consensus.

Vancouver's rejection of the Nairobi Assembly's Just, Participatory and Sustainable Society reflects, in part, the impatience of the Third World

13 Warwick Fox, 'Towards a Deeper Ecology?' in *Habitat Australia*, Vol. 13, No. 4, August 1985, p. 26.

with sustainability interpreted as the maintenance of unjust international structures. JPIC, on the other hand, seems to represent a much more thoroughgoing rejection of the whole idea of a global society in favour of regional associations, which may explain, for example, why the Basle JPIC Assembly was much more successful than the JPIC World Congress in Seoul. JPIC is, in essence, a 'bottom up' approach which will never offer a blueprint for the kind of global society hankered after by the ecumenical *ancien régime*.

And similarly with theology. For centuries a handful of theological traditions have been handed down and grafted onto cultures many of which themselves contain rich resources capable of enabling the churches to respond to current problems. It is to these resources that we now turn.

The following examples are mostly taken from contributions by participants to WCC consultations, which are listed for convenience together with those already mentioned in Table I.

The importance of creation as the cornerstone of any attempt to free African Christianity from western influence has been described by the Ghanaian theologian, John Pobee, as follows:

It is inadequate to have Africans appropriate completely the North Atlantic statement of theology without any adjustment and reference to their own context. Therefore the first task of African Christian theology regarding creation is how to free theology from its captivity and to use African insights and experience to express the biblical insights about creation . . . In the African context the evil in the creation which was created good is not an academic issue. It is a matter of survival of peoples in the Sahel, in Tanzania, in South Africa.[14]

The question of survival in the face of drought has been taken up by the Justice and Peace Commission for the Catholic Church of Ghana, which has published a study of desertification calling upon Church and State to make every practical effort to preserve the God-given legacy of a land rich in natural resources 'for the sake of generations unborn'.[15] Many Ghanaian taboos and customs are designed either to preserve nature or to maintain a balance between people and nature – thus fishermen cannot fish on Tuesdays because that is the ocean's day of rest.

Mrs Adebisi Sowunmi, professor of paleontology at the University of Ibadan in Nigeria, summarised traditional African affinity between

14 John Pobee, 'Creation, the Most Important Task for a Theology of Creation Today', forthcoming.
15 *Desertification of Ghana*, Justice and Peace Commission of the Catholic Church of Ghana, September 1982.

humanity and nature at the Amsterdam consultation on 'Reintegrating God's Creation' as follows:

Creation is a single dynamic entity whose component parts are closely interwoven and interdependent. The wholeness and oneness, i.e. the integrity of creation, was duly recognised by early humans . . . Communities of primary agriculturalists . . . also maintain the integrity of creation, their farms of mixed crops being very similar to the natural forest ecosystem which has a great diversity of plant species.[16]

Jesse Mugambi, professor of religious studies at Nairobi University, and a member of the Church and Society Working Committee, stresses the importance of 'relationship' as a distinctive African category which, he claims, is at least as important as the Baluba concept of 'vital force' or John Mbiti's notion of time:

All Africans in traditional life believe that nothing can be well with them if a good relationship is not maintained between them and all the powers which are perceived in the environment. These include God, [other people], ancestors, established institutions, and ritual animals, plants, non-living objects and special places. If the relationship is broken, then it must be restored before the situation can return to normal.[17]

South African theologian Allan Boesak stresses the biblical covenant between humanity and nature, an understanding which is central to Reformed Theology.

God says we are here to rule over the earth and to cultivate it, but our power over the earth only makes sense in terms of the covenant – that is, in terms of our servanthood . . . I recall hearing about an African tribe which made their boats from tree trunks, but before they cut down the tree, they spoke to it, explaining their need for a boat. Then they waited several days to give the spirit of the tree a chance to find a new home. After a respectful time they returned and cut down the tree. In former times we called this animism or heathen belief. Now it is called ecology.[18]

During a JPIC preparatory meeting in Geneva, Joe Seremane, also from South Africa, commented on the similarities between the recommendations of the Manila consultation and comparable South African issues

16 Adebisi Sowunmi, 'How and why creation disintegrated', in *Reintegrating God's Creation*, Church and Society Documents, No. 3, September 1987, p. 11.

17 Jesse Mugambi, *God, humanity and nature in relation to justice and peace*, Church and Society Documents, No. 2, September 1987, p. (ii).

18 *Forum*, JPIC Newsletter, No. 6, May 1989, p. 1.

which, he maintained, possess an immediacy not always appreciated in the West:

> The things which threaten peace and justice in communities under threat go hand in hand with overcrowding, which results in the rapid denudation of occupied land, an obvious attack on the 'integrity of creation' which is a far more immediate threat than acid rain or chemical or nuclear pollution.[19]

In a contribution to the Annecy consultation on theocentric ethics, Gabriel Setiloane, professor of religious studies in the University of Cape Town, suggested ways in which traditional African world views might enhance our relationship with nature. These are: notions about the beginnings of life which imply a common origin for people and animals, 'sustained by the same Mother Earth and harnessed together by the same natural elements, sharing life together in the wholeness of community'; understanding of the totality of a community in which 'success in life is found in the ability to maintain a healthy relationship with all'; and an animistic view of God which comes close to panentheism (i.e. the view that God works in and through the world):

> We in Africa have a sense of religion and seem to agree more with philosopher scientists like Sir Alister Hardy . . . We are not talking pantheism. Recently, thanks to John Robinson, a new term has entered Western theological parlance: *panentheism*. We ask then; what difference is it to *animism* understood from inside by a very religious people?[20]

We shall take up this issue again in chapter four.

Enough has been said to indicate that African thought contains a variety of distinctive understandings of creation from which the churches can draw in order to respond to the current environmental crises.

There are a number of similarities between African thought and Latin American liberation theology. South American native Indians believe that all land is held in possession from God, and is a gift. Creation is automatically taken to mean both the people and the land, and is implicit in the situation of the people. It is not unusual in, say, a Brazilian eucharist for the offertory to include not only bread and wine, but flowers, wheat, seeds, water and many other things which symbolise our relationship with the land. The São Paulo consultation produced an attractive liturgy based on the seven days of creation incorporating many such ideas.[21]

19 Joe Seremane, 'The Covenant Project' in the *Ecumenical Review*, Vol. 38, No. 3, WCC Geneva, July 1986, p. 340.
20 Gabriel M. Setiloane, 'Towards a biocentric theology and ethic, via Africa', Annecy consultation (1988), p. 13.
21 'And God saw that it was good . . .', WCC, Geneva, 1989.

In addition to such traditional influences, liberation theology has also come to recognise that justice for the poor cannot be achieved without regard to their physical circumstances, and that the liberation of people must be accompanied by the liberation of all life. Philosopher Mary Midgley described this change of emphasis at the São Paulo consultation as follows:

> The further change that is now happening [in liberation theology] is the realisation that the liberation of nature, too, is a necessary part of the same Christian enterprise. God's creation is not just our convenience-food, a mass of raw material to be opened up and consumed at our fancy. 'Creation Theology' – supplementing liberation theology – points out that, to the contrary, we have to take it entirely seriously as an end in itself. Nature is neither our tool nor a rival competing with us. It is simply the whole within which we, as one created species, form a part.[22]

Just as Gabriel Setiloane finds echoes of modern philosophy and science in traditional African thought, so liberation theologians discover similarities between the beliefs of indigenous Indians and notions such as the 'liberation of life' used by process philosophers and theologians.

Asian religious thought presupposes a much greater degree of closeness between humanity and nature than is generally accepted in the West. Thus, for example, when news of Darwinism reached nineteenth-century India, the reaction of educated Hindus was entirely favourable; did not the gods assume the form of animals, and could not all of us, in theory at any rate, be reborn in other life forms?

The same thread runs through the Gandhian notions of non-violence to all life (*ahimsā*) and *sarvodaya* (literally, the awakening of all), a view of development based on decentralised and highly participative village republics which, though not directed primarily at solving environmental problems, represent an integrated vision with a more benign attitude to nature than that of governments and planners.[23] Gandhi's distaste for wasteful western patterns of development is legendary. 'What do you think of western civilisation?', he was once asked. 'I think it would be a good idea', the Mahatma replied.

Sarvodaya also forms the basis of A. T. Ariyaratne's Buddhist version of Gandhian development in Sri Lanka. Among its novel features are the use of sailcloth windmills made by fishing communities and strengthened

22 Mary Midgley, *Church and Society Newsletter*, No. 11, October 1988, p. 2.
23 David Gosling, 'Religion and the Environment', in Angell, Comer and Wilkinson, eds., *Sustaining Earth*, Macmillan, 1990, p. 100.

with a special dye. These serve the double function of producing electricity in an environmentally-friendly manner and providing work for poor fisherfolk who in Sri Lanka as elsewhere have been badly hit by technologically sophisticated Japanese and European trawlers plying their coasts.

Thai Buddhism has recently produced some imaginative programmes which combine environmentally-sensitive development with primary health care and the use of herbal medicines. The practitioners are monks who justify such activities with reference to Buddhist scriptures as the rediscovery of an ancient role.[24]

Distinctive church responses to the environmental crises in Asia have so far been few. The theological dimension of the Manila consultation was addressed by Kim Yong Bock, co-director of the Third World Leadership Training Centre in Korea. According to Kim, justice and peace are best understood and interpreted to us by those who experience their absence. Thus, he argues from his characteristically Minjung perspective, it is through the suffering of the victims of oppression – environmental, technological or whatever – that new insights are gained, new possibilities emerge:

> The victims of power and technology hold privileged knowledge not understood by the experts, the scientists, the academics. For they hold an epistemological advantage. The victims have a special knowledge and experience of history, real history, of which those who control are completely unaware. The Biblical message must be understood as the account of what God is doing in the world through its victims. The reality is that the Bible is not an account of the experience of the privileged in society but that of its victims . . .

> Christian community as the ecumenical movement for justice, peace and integrity of creation is a movement to cultivate justice, koinonia (fellowship) and shalom in the universe. In this context we recognize that the subject of the gardening work is the people of God, and at the same time all created things, not merely humans, are participants in the Garden.[25]

The following Filipino version of the Stations of the Cross is a graphic demonstration of the way liturgy can communicate important ecological insights:

24 David Gosling, 'Visions of Salvation: A Thai Buddhist Experience of Ecumenism', in Modern Asian Studies, Vol. 26, No. 1, Cambridge University Press, 1992, p. 31.
25 Kim Yong Bock, 'Justice, Peace and the Integrity of Creation', in Carino and Gosling, Op. cit. (7), p. 48.

Jesus turned to those weeping and said: 'Weep not for me but for yourselves and your children, because the day will come when the people will say to the mountains, "Fall on us", for if such things as these are done when the forest is green what will happen when it is a desert . . . ?' After the burial of Jesus there is a fifteenth station: the Resurrection. After the death of the rain forest there is no resurrection. The forest will not return to life.[26]

We shall consider a regional response from the Pacific in the next chapter and the 'regional' responses of Orthodoxy, especially Russian Orthodoxy, in chapter four, together with some more theological developments based in Europe. Before concluding this chapter, however, we must mention eco-justice, which for some churches in the USA is virtually synonymous with JPIC.

The eco-justice group in North America came into being when two bodies dealing primarily with the churches' response to acid rain in the USA and Canada joined forces in October 1984. Initially, as representatives of the two national church councils tried to reconcile the need to stop pollution from acid rain with the prospect of putting thousands of miners of high sulphur coal out of work, ecological sustainability and justice seemed to be in conflict. But as time went on and alternative employment possibilities for redundant miners were created, a number of highly effective task forces were set up in both countries to monitor and combat air and water pollution.

William E. Gibson, coordinator of the Eco-Justice Project, explains eco-justice as follows:

Eco-justice means both ecological wholeness and social justice – never one without the other. Eco-justice extends the concept of justice to the earth as well as to people . . . Its power reflects nature's claim – and the Creator's claim – upon the human creature to respect the integrity and honour the intrinsic worth of the whole created order.[27]

Eco-justice represents a move away from the pragmatic instrumentalism adopted towards nature by North Atlantic liberals during the 1970s in favour of the view that nature possesses internal limits:

Given the threats to the creation that exist today, the central challenge to theologians is to resolve this question: Is a creation-wide 'new life' – a profound change in human nature –

26 *Death of a Forest*, Columban Mission, Manila, n.d., p. 2, available in Britain as a slide and audio meditation from CAFOD.
27 William E. Gibson, editorial in *The Egg*, Quarterly Journal of Eco-Justice, Vol. 5, No. 2, 1985.

theoretically possible? Do the events remembered on Good Friday and Easter offer hope for the whole creation as well as the individual? Or are we collectively still in bondage to sin, the creation condemned to continue groaning?[28]

Finally, from the USA, a feminist response by Sallie McFague, who contributed a striking paper 'Imaging a Theology of Nature: The World as God's Body' to the theocentric ethics consultation at Annecy:

What this experiment with the world as God's body comes to . . . is an awareness, both chilling and breathtaking, that we, as worldly, bodily beings, are in God's presence. We do not have to go to some special place . . . to find God, for God is present with us here and now. We have a basis for a revived sacramentalism, that is, a perception of the divine as visible, as present, palpably present in the world. But it is a kind of sacramentalism that is painfully conscious of the world's vulnerability, its preciousness, its uniqueness. The beauty of the world and its ability to sustain the vast multitude of species it supports is not there for the taking. The world is a body that must be carefully tended, that must be nurtured, protected, guided, loved, and befriended both as valuable in itself – for like us, it is an expression of God – and as necessary to the continuation of life . . . .In the metaphor of the world as God's body the resurrection is remythologised as a worldly, present, inclusive event – the offering of the world, God's body, to all: 'This is my body'.[29]

These are some of the theological and religious responses to the environmental crises during the past few years. Just as the form in which environmental problems have appeared in different parts of the world has varied from region to region, so the most fruitful responses have been those which incorporate local cultural and religious traditions, especially in relation to views about creation. And whether one considers environmental issues on their own, or together with the kind of responses we have given as examples, questions concerning justice, and to a lesser extent, peace, are invariably in evidence.

In the next chapter we shall consider a series of responses to particular crises in order to further illustrate the links between justice, peace and the integrity of creation.

28 Gerald O. Barney, 'The Future of the Creation', in *The Egg*, Quarterly Jounal of Eco-Justice, Vol. 5, No. 3, 1985, p. 5.
29 Sallie McFague, 'Imaging a Theology of Nature: The World as God's Body', in Birch, Eakin and McDaniel, eds., *Liberating Life*, Orbis Books, 1990, p. 217.

3 Responding to Crises

Between 1984 and 1989 the WCC made a number of important statements about major environmental issues. Some of these were short responses to disasters, such as occurred at Bhopal and Chernobyl; others, such as the team visit to the Marshall Islands in 1987 were based on more sustained research. AIDS has an environmental dimension in that it influences our social behaviour; the WCC's response is therefore included in this chapter. As in the last chapter, each example has a major environmental component – usually the point of entry – which quickly leads into areas of justice and peace.

(i) Marshalls team visit

Delegates to the Vancouver Assembly were profoundly shocked to learn of the long-term effects of fallout from the 1950's nuclear bomb tests in the Pacific. Darlene Keju-Johnson, a young health care worker from the Marshall Islands, gave a disturbing account of genetic malfunctions which had produced babies which looked more like jellyfish than humans. She herself has had several radiation-induced cancers removed.

In October 1987 a small WCC team paid a ten-day visit to the Marshalls with the two-fold brief to assess ongoing health care programmes and plans, and to promote improved understanding and advocacy for efforts to improve health in the Marshall Islands. The team visit followed an invitation to the WCC by the Marshalls Health Minister, Tony de Brum, and was organised jointly by the Christian Medical Commission and Church and Society.

Team members were Erlinda Senturias, director of National Ecumenical Health Concerns in the Philippines (team leader), Charles Kerr, professor of preventative and social medicine at the University of Sydney and a Fellow of the Royal College of Surgeons, Bernard Lau, an ethnically Chinese family doctor in Toronto, and the associate director and director of the two sub-units. Darlene and Giff Keju-Johnson and Majuro Hospital staff coordinated the programme.

In spite of the seriousness of the effects of nuclear fallout on some islanders, it was decided to study this problem within the context of the islands' overall health needs. This was partly because the US Government scheme for compensating fallout victims, Compact 177, had been so abused that people receiving compensation were regarded with great hostility by those who were not. In such a divisive situation it seemed best to study the overall health needs of all the islanders, recognising that some were related to nuclear fallout while others were the ones normally associated with underdevelopment. From the point of view of our understanding of JPIC, we can see how an inadequate 'justice' response to an earlier environmental catastrophe was responsible for an infringement of peace in terms of social divisions; here, as elsewhere, true justice means much more than financial remuneration!

The geography and history of the Marshall Islands require amplification. Thirty-four atolls covering 500,000 square miles are populated by 37,000 Marshallese, half of whom are under the age of fourteen. Whereas the outer islands are among the least densely populated parts of the world, the tiny island of Ebeye, where some 9,000 Marshallese inhabit a 70-acre strip, is one of the most densely populated. This is because the entire populations of islands such as Bikini and Enewetok moved because of the nuclear tests to where they might find employment at Kwajalein military base, two miles from Ebeye. The international date line runs between Majuro and Kwajalein, the world's largest atoll.

Following a period of trusteeship under the UN, the Marshalls entered into a Compact of Free Association with the Kwajalein missile base. MX and other missiles are fired into the sea around Kwajalein from a range of 4,000 miles away in California, and plans are being considered for Star Wars missile hardware to be deposited in the same area. The US Government is considering using the site to bury nuclear waste.

Between 1946 and 1958, the USA carried out twenty-three atmospheric nuclear tests on Bikini and forty-three assorted nuclear tests on Enewetok. In March 1954 the largest hydrogen bomb ever tested, 'Bravo', unleashed more explosive force than all the combined wars in history. Some islands were totally destroyed and have disappeared from the map. During the Manila consultation Darlene Keju-Johnson described what it was like to grow up in the Marshalls:

> I grew up on an island 300 miles downwind of Bikini Atoll. As a child I remember seeing the flash from one of the many tests. Like many other Marshallese, I have fears about my health. Already I have had surgery to remove two tumours, and I have more that must be removed . . . Our fish are increasingly poisonous, and our arrowroot, a staple food for Marshallese (like a potato), has completely disappeared from the northern islands. Many of our breadfruits are half-brown and half-green and often inedible.
>
> People have a fear that almost every health problem is caused by radiation. It is becoming a big psychological problem for Marshallese people. The other fear is where people are going to go if their islands are contaminated. Our islands are very small

but they are our only home . . . Our own Marshallese doctors have no knowledge of radiation – they don't understand the health problems that result from exposure to radioactivity. So we have to rely on US government doctors who tell us not to worry, that everything is OK – even when we know it is not.

We Marshallese have already had a preview of World War Three. We've had sixty-six atomic and hydrogen bombs dropped on our islands by the USA; six islands have been blown off the face of the earth.[30]

It was this kind of information from the Pacific which shocked the Vancouver delegates, especially those from the USA, most of whom had no idea of what had been happening in their former colony.

Darlene's references to fear and psychological problems were borne out by the team visit. Security was often used to justify withholding information about illness, and inasmuch as many of the medical tests for cancers were carried out in Hawaii, it was impossible to check the results. One of the team's recommendations was that such testing could be carried out much less expensively in Fiji or even Australia, or that Marshallese hospitals could be upgraded to make such journeys unnecessary. But a major reason for severing the US/Hawaii link was to give Marshallese right of access to their own health information. Lack of reliable information about such matters contributed to the islanders' fears and feelings of inadequacy, which were reflected in a number of severe social problems such as a high suicide rate among the young (ten deaths during the first six months of 1987).

Seventy per cent of the islanders are Protestant, mostly affiliated to the United Church of Christ (UCC) in the USA, the rest are Roman Catholic (15%) or members of various sects. There is no council of churches, and the United Church recently split into two sections, making it difficult for the visiting team to work with them. The Roman Catholics and Assemblies of God were supportive of the visit, and although the UCC showed little official interest, Darlene and the Youth-to-Youth group, all of whom are practising members, played a major role.

(ii) **Access to health**

The team held extensive discussions with personnel at the Majuro and Ebeye hospitals and met representatives from the Health Ministry and various US departments. A meeting was held with radiation-affected

30 Darlene Keju-Johnson, 'Nuclearisation and Militarisation in the Pacific', in Feliciano Carino and David Gosling, eds., *Technology from the Underside'*, NCCP, 1986, p. 30.

people from Rongelap, and visits were made to outer island dispensaries in Laura and Bikarej.

The team's report begins by stating as a fundamental issue of justice the right of everyone to equal access to the Marshallese health care system.[31] Practical obstacles include the geography of the islands and the distribution of population among them, cultural and social differences between city and outer island Marshallese and the special needs of people from the four 'radiation exposed' atolls – continuing health care for whom is proving a divisive and counter-productive social and political issue.

The second and third sections of the report deal with the application of available health services according to perceived needs and community participation in the provision of health services. These sections recognise that outside 'experts' have been telling the Marshallese how to run their health but that to act on the basis of such an approach is incompatible with our fundamental understanding of what health and wholeness are all about. The only genuine and permanent solution is for the Marshallese to take their health into their own hands, which will in the long run mean that primary health care must be given systematic priority over the present emphasis on curative hospital services which eat up 59% of the total health budget.

Thus people's participation is set out as the means for achieving justice in relation both to the problems of fallout victims and the islanders as a whole. The third section of the report gives examples of the work of women's and youth groups in facilitating health care, and recognises the enormous potential role of the churches. This is followed by a section examining the respective roles of the public and private sectors in primary health care and the need for integration and coordinated action.

The report's fifth section looks at the distinctive problems posed by radioactive fallout. It begins by analysing the history of the Compact 177 compensation plan, so named on account of its position in a US Government document. This was originally conceived to assist 176 officially designated victims of nuclear radiation, but the number has grown to 8260 partly because some radiation-induced cancers took a long time to develop, but also because everyone wanted to jump onto the compensation bandwagon with the result that the incentive to be classified as sick outweighed the desire to be regarded as healthy.

At this point the report trenchantly states that 'the cultural and social dislocations from the tests can indirectly affect health and wellbeing in excess of direct damage induced by radiation'. Even so there remain many

31 *Your Health is in Your Hands,* Church and Society Documents, No. 8, October 1988, and *Church and Society Newsletter,* No. 9, April 1988.

major uncertainties about the long-term effects of fallout, and the report recognises that data from the Chernobyl accident suggests that air-borne radioactivity spreads much less evenly than previously appreciated. The section concludes by calling for more participation in decision-making on the part of people from the four radiation-exposed atolls, further unbiased studies in the region which take into account the Chernobyl data, and a complete rethinking of the Compact 177 plan so that people have more incentive to get well than to remain or become dependent on an expensive, ineffective and socially divisive scheme.

During the final debriefing the team members discussed the report with the Minister of Health and his staff. It was agreed that within an overall context of moving from secondary, curative health services based on the two hospitals in the direction of primary health care, specialised tertiary services might be transferred from Hawaii to Majuro hospital. Thus tests for thyroid cancer disorders carried out under conditions of secrecy in the USA would routinely be carried out in the Marshalls. It was accepted by the Minister that this could be done.

The following recommendations were agreed:

(i) There is a heavy concentration of health activities centred on Majuro and Ebeye hospitals, and a lack of adequately maintained dispensaries on the outer islands. This imbalance must be redressed within the context of an overall shift away from curative medicine to primary health care. Compact 177 must be reviewed.

(ii) Political leverage must be brought to bear on the US Congress to allow open access by Marshallese to the results of all medical tests carried out on them since nuclear testing began, and access to the US courts to redress claims for injury.

The team expressed appreciation to the Youth-to-Youth in Health programme led by Roma Beijiko for its success in communicating health information throughout the islands. But it was critical of a scheme proposed by Operation Mobilisation to supply a ship staffed by medical students from the USA to travel around the islands – Darlene angrily pointed out that this would make the Marshallese almost as much guinea pigs as flying them to US hospitals for tests for cancers!

Both the visiting team and the Ministry of Health acknowledged that primary health care is preferable to curative services because it provides more people with a greater degree of access to health care, and does so in a participative manner which avoids the dependencies which are inevitable in hospitals – the same applies elsewhere, including Britain. But having acknowledged that the first recommendation is based on sound health policy, it cannot be denied that the attempt to push both secondary and tertiary health care in the direction of primary health care had a political edge to it (because it removed responsibility for cancer tests from US doctors in Hawaii). The same could be said about the Youth-to-Youth group's ban on drinking Coca-Cola, which, though sound health policy, was also a protest against the USA.

The demand for access to medical records from the US Congress and an end to secrecy about medical tests is essentially an extension of the first recommendation. If individuals and communities are to take responsibility for their own health, then they must have access to all relevant data. Therefore, if the Marshallese Government is to plan for the future of its people, justice requires that it must have access to the results of all medical tests conducted on the victims of nuclear fallout. Remuneration may go some way towards redressing the wrongs of the past, but it does not buy secrecy. But powerful Governments are remarkably reluctant to part with such information: the British Government was no exception following its nuclear tests in Australia.

The political context of the visit was extremely delicate. We were told by our hosts not to make any political criticisms of the USA. Some WCC colleagues in Geneva were shocked that we went at all under such compromising circumstances – was it not our clear duty to denounce the USA for its neo-colonialism and militarisation in the region? In the event the Marshallese had the right to set our terms of reference, and did so. They wanted to know how, from the perspective of justice, we would resolve an internal 'peace' issue arising from the division of islanders into factions as a result of a flawed scheme for compensating victims of nuclear fallout. We equated justice with equal right of access to health care and people's participation as the means to attain it. But the right of people to determine their own future – to secure justice for the next generation – entitles them to access to all relevant information, some of which could only be obtained with the agreement of the US Congress. What could be more innocently and reasonably 'non-political' than that?

The team visit and its conclusions are an illuminating example of how an environmental point of entry into a problem moves swiftly into the areas of peace and justice, and how a participatory and inclusive commitment to justice can offer a positive way forward. The statements made by the team arising from the visit were of a moral type which can be appreciated and acted upon by governments. The notions of justice between generations and a people's rights to determine their own future are soundly ethical, similar in some respects to the *Brundtland Report*'s concept of sustainable development, while the call to the US Congress to provide access to medical records is a non-ideological policy type of moral statement of a kind which governments can usually act upon, however reluctantly.

The Marshall Islands were not the only part of the Pacific to receive attention, and Céline Hoiore-Atger from French Polynesia gave a moving account of the effects of French nuclear testing on Mururoa Atoll at a special public forum organised by Church and Society towards the end of the 1988 Central Committee in Hanover. Her address was a straightforward plea for an end to testing in the region. Ironically it seems that the Protestant churches in France are more solidly opposed to nuclear testing than some Pacific church members in the region, who, Céline claims, have been provided with inadequate information and simply bought off with large sums of money.

The recommendations of the Marshalls team visit were brought to the attention of the Hanover Central Committee and also the JPIC regional meeting which took place in Western Samoa in 1988. They were communicated to the National Council of Churches of the USA and to Episcopalian Presiding Bishop Edmund Browning, who as a former bishop of Hawaii has a strong commitment to a nuclear-free Pacific. They were also noted and acted upon by the Canberra Assembly.

(iii) **License to kill?**

On December 3rd 1984, the release of toxic gases from a Union Carbide plant at Bhopal in India killed an estimated 2500 people and maimed another 10,000 to 200,000. This was the worst ever industrial disaster.

The tragedy spoke for itself and no statement from the WCC in Geneva seemed necessary. But a year later some churches in India were concerned at the inadequacy of Union Carbide's offer of compensation, while Union Carbide itself was looking for ways of re-establishing public confidence and in this mood approached the WCC to ask if it would provide a forum for a discussion of the ethical aspects of the disaster. At the same time the WCC received a request from a Bombay-based film team to show their film of the disaster 'License to Kill'. It was decided to show the film and invite Union Carbide and the Indian government representative to the UN to respond. The film was duly shown, but the Union Carbide delegate became so angry that he would not go onto the platform.

Shortly after the meeting WCC General Secretary Emilio Castro released the following statement:

> On the anniversary of the Bhopal tragedy, we join people around the world in sorrow and recognise that commercially motivated development causes unacceptable loss of life and avoidable ill health. We believe that God calls us not only to care for the victims but to change our ways.
>
> Trade unions, citizens' associations and Asian churches remind us forcefully that on December 3, 1984, thousands died in Bhopal

and tens of thousands are irretrievably handicapped. We remember their sufferings in our prayers. Although some of the victims have received minimal financial assistance and further compensation can be expected through the courts, much more needs to be done to rehabilitate the community as a whole, and to prevent similar disasters occurring elsewhere in the future.

Recognising the promises and the risks of the enormous resources available through the development of the chemical industry, we call upon all people of goodwill to urge governments and trans-national corporations to heed these voices of conscience. The background to the disaster was researched by Cécile de Sweemer, a Belgian doctor and public health expert.[32] Her recommendations were as follows:

(i) There is an urgent need to follow up the long-term effects of the tragedy. These include the rehabilitation of the community as a whole, and not just the giving of money and medical assistance to those who most appear to need it.

(ii) Within the overall context of rehabilitation, priority should be given to women and children and to the creation of employment for handicapped people.

(iii) On the basis of evidence at our disposal . . . we do not believe that the disaster was the result of sabotage; we maintain that Union Carbide must use a different method of chemical processing and a different safety design.

(iv) In the future Union Carbide should try to cultivate a more positive relationship with unions and community groups, recognising that they fulfil a positive role and assist communication.

(v) In the future more information must be readily available to employees, physicians and to the local community.

There are similarities between these recommendations and some of the points raised in the last section in connection with the Marshalls. Rehabilitation means more than throwing money at people, or even money plus healthcare; it means 'peace', the state of a healthy society. Physicians, people in general, must have right of access to information.

But the statement does not come down against technological development, or even commercially motivated development; it is the balancing of commercial gain against risk to human health and safety that is crucial. And although India possesses a fine record of environmental and health legislation, it does not have the infrastructure to maintain these in far-

32 Cécile de Sweemer, 'The Bhopal Industrial Disaster', in Carino and Gosling, Op. cit. (28), p. 58.

flung areas. Among the causes of the disaster for which the Government of India should take responsibility, we listed the licensing of the plant and choice of an urban site, the ignoring of warning signs, and the lack of information about safety procedures on the part of almost everybody from the police to the unions.

But underlying the causes of the Bhopal disaster is the fact that the commercial push for pesticides in developing countries is part of a series of linkages whereby unjust international structures increasingly force people and land to produce more and more cash crops for export to pay debts to bodies like the International Monetary Fund (IMF) and the World Bank.

(iv) Chernobyl

The Chernobyl nuclear disaster in May 1986 received immediate attention from the WCC on account of the insistent, though muted concern of the Russian Orthodox Church. The directors of Church and Society and the Churches' Commission on International Affairs drafted a joint statement for the General Secretary, as follows:

As we send you greetings in the name of Christ, we convey through you our sympathy for all victims of the accident at the nuclear plant at Chernobyl in the Ukraine. The people in the Soviet Union and those in other countries affected by nuclear radiation have been very much in our thoughts and prayers these days.

The accident has come as yet another sombre reminder of the grave risks involved in the production and use of nuclear energy. The WCC has maintained that there are serious unresolved questions associated with reactor safety, appropriate safeguards for radiation protection and effective international standards. It has called for public debate in all countries about the overall risks, costs and benefits of nuclear energy.

The accident has underlined the need for all nations to accept improved arrangements for regular inspection by appropriate international agencies for the maintenance of the safety of nuclear plants.

In view of the fact that radiation quickly spreads across nations, there is need for expeditious and full sharing of information on matters related to safety of nuclear reactors.

As we continue to uphold you and all the people in your country in our intercessions, we express our readiness to assist you in all possible ways.

At the time of the accident members of Church and Society were in York attempting to provide a theological interpretation of the phrase 'integrity of creation' with a group from the Faith and Order sub-unit. As the York participants discussed 'ambiguity in creation, contingency, freedom, sin, limits, and "New Creation",' the two directors responsible for the statement argued about whether, in the wake of Chernobyl, it was still possible to speak of the risks *and* benefits of nuclear power.

A few days after the disaster a member of the New Zealand Dairy Board phoned to ask for information about consequent levels of radioactivity in different parts of Europe. Were they as high as during the nuclear tests of the fifties? Why were the International Atomic Energy Agency and the World Health Organisation unable to provide any data? Answers to these questions were obtained from a member of the Birmingham Radiation Centre and the editorial staff of the *New Scientist*.

When the Chernobyl disaster was discussed at the following Church and Society Working Committee in Potsdam, some members were visibly unnerved by it, and Pirkko Penttila, a nuclear scientist and a member of the Finnish Orthodox Church, explained how she had almost resigned her job after the disaster. Brian Wynne, director of the Centre for Science Studies and Science Policy at Lancaster University, conducted an analysis of the accident in which he urged the churches to affirm many positive elements in the tragedy, such as the unprecedented levels of cooperation between Russian scientists and their western counterparts. In the course of a public hearing at the 1987 Central Committee in Geneva, Archbishop Kirill of Smolensk described his feelings during a car journey to the site of the disaster shortly after it occurred:

> For many of us Chernobyl was a kind of moral challenge. It somehow burst into our everyday life. It demanded immediate actions and great sacrifice. It influenced the thinking of many people. Many people began to think what does it mean to give one's own life for others. Many people suffered and gave their life for others. This was an impulse for moral and ethical thinking . . . And the Church tried to find its place in these deliberations. Our hierarchy made several statements concerning Chernobyl. I also made one. And we organised a campaign for collecting money which was used to help refugees.[33]

By the time the Church and Society Working Committee met in September 1988 in Tambov, in the former USSR, Chernobyl was largely forgotten, and the blossoming of 'perestroika' had created a mood in which both Church and society were willing to explore environmental issues

33 *Church and Society Newsletter*, No. 6, May 1987.

together. But our Orthodox hosts – Metropolitan Philaret of Minsk and Bishop Feofan of Kashira – clearly had appreciated the non-confrontational form of our Chernobyl statement. It had enabled them to discuss nuclear power with their own Government, and although the risks had been emphasised, benefits remained a future possibility.

Russia's enormous dependency on electricity, and therefore in the long run on less polluting alternatives to coal, is clearly apparent in the vast arrays of pylons on the outskirts of Moscow and St Petersburg – a testimony to Lenin's celebrated view that 'Communism is socialism plus electrification'.

(v) **World Environment Day**

On June 5th 1986, at the request of the United Nations Environment Programme (UNEP), the WCC hosted a meeting at which representatives of international Christian, Muslim and Jewish organisations celebrated World Environment Day with prepared statements and a panel discussion.

Speaking on behalf of the World Jewish Congress, Gerhart Riegner, its co-chair, stressed the links between protecting the environment and the quest for peace. Quoting from the Hebrew Bible, he explained the Levitical injunction to give the land a sabbath, or jubilee rest every seven years, and the custom of celebrating the new year of trees:

There are very specific and original institutions in the old Jewish tradition that bear witness to the deep concern of the Jewish people for the environment. And while the institutions of the sabbatical year and of the jubilee year are today mainly of a symbolic character, they are particularly significant in this respect.

Let me quote from Leviticus 25:2–5: 'When you come to the land which I give you, then shall the land keep a sabbath to the Lord. Six years thou shalt sow thy field, and six years thou shalt prune thy vineyard, and gather in its fruit; but in the seventh year there shall be a sabbath of solemn rest for the land, a sabbath for the Lord; thou shalt neither sow thy field nor prune thy vineyard. That which grows of its own accord of thy harvest thou shalt not reap, nor gather the grapes of thy undressed vine: for it shall be a year of rest for the land' . . . The rule shows a very specific concept of property: the concept of God's ownership of the land.

I would like to mention another Jewish custom, which has been observed over the centuries and which is observed up to our days: the celebration of the festival of the new year of trees, *Tu bishvat*, at which we celebrate the renewal of nature. It is customary to eat at this occasion fifteen kinds of fruit and to recite the psalms that praise the creation. It is the day when Jewish school children plant trees – as we are doing today. Moreover, in modern times this day has become the symbol of the revival and redemption of the land by the conquest of the desert. Let me remind you in this respect that the planting of millions of trees, the unprecedented effort of afforestation and the programmes of the desert research institutes belong to the most significant achievements of the young State of Israel.

Representing the World Muslim Congress, Abdul H. Tabibi also stressed the links between peace and the environment:

If you read the Quran you may observe that Islam is a structure of peace and its most outstanding principle is peace and submission to the one and only God.

Peace with Allah and peace with man and the world at large, that is the whole environment. Peace with Allah implies complete submission to His will, and peace with man implies the doing of good to fellow men and refraining from doing any injury or evil to them; certainly it includes also not doing any injury to the environment in which man lives and gets his shelter, food and happiness.

He also described God as the owner, sustainer and life-giver of people, animals and plants, and emphasised our responsibilities to the environment.

The Vatican had indicated its willingness on this occasion to be represented by the WCC. General Secretary Emilio Castro read a statement, from which the following is an extract:

Each religion has its specific teachings that seek to further the human search for peace with God, with oneself, one's neighbour, peace among nations and a responsible stewardship by human beings of creation, and peace between all creatures and the human race. Christians share with Jews and Muslims the common biblical tradition which covers all these concepts by the word *shalom*. God's *shalom* cannot manifest itself to those who do not obey his command of justice. This theme is strongly reflected in the gospels, and flowered again in the thirteenth century, most significantly with St. Francis of Assisi. All Christian traditions have preserved its memory.

We affirm science and technology as gifts from God that need to be used with humility and discipline for the service of people and for the preservation and restoration of healthy self-sustaining ecologies. Peace and the integrity of creation are more than ever threatened by the irresponsible use of technology by individuals and communities. A transformation of technology will be a necessary, but not a sufficient step towards peace and the restoration of the integrity of creation. That will call for a much greater seriousness of purpose on the part of nations, communities and individuals, a commitment to pursue justice between people and between nations. It asks that we dedicate human technology and all human endeavours to the common good rather than to the exclusive benefit of some.

The statement went on to recall the Bhopal and Chernobyl disasters and other threats to the environment such as deforestation. It appealed for renewed hope and an urgent review of our lifestyles, concluding with this declaration:

We Christians believe that God sent his Son to save all of creation that is in travail. We believe that God sustains and loves all living beings and the universe itself. As his children and heirs we cannot refuse our responsibility . . . Let us therefore rededicate ourselves and pray that we may be worthy of the task and join hands with our brothers and sisters in Judaism, Islam and other religions, as well as in secular humanism, and labour together to restore and preserve the integrity of creation.

In spite of the high level of importance given to this occasion, the UN gardeners would not allow a token tree to be planted before the autumn. This part of the ceremony was therefore conducted on October 24th 1986, when most of the people who had been on the panel were not available. But a small group of dedicated representatives from the three religions gathered outside the UN library and took turns to shovel soil onto the roots of a large and rather ungainly tree. The WCC was represented by the director of Church and Society, who on that particular occasion represented both the four hundred million members of the member churches of the WCC, and the entire Roman Catholic Church!

(vi) AIDS

AIDS came onto the ecumenical agenda because the World Health Organisation (WHO) complained to the World Council of Churches that certain fundamentalist churches in the USA were blocking research grants for AIDS because they claimed that the disease was God's judgement on homosexuals and therefore should be allowed to run its course. The US Episcopalians and Canadian Anglicans also approached the WCC to say that they would welcome a study of the disease and the best way for the churches to respond to it.

Early in 1986, the General Secretary asked Church and Society to brief him on the subject in time for the March WCC Executive in Zaire, where the disease had first been clearly identified, and was known to be passed on by heterosexual transmission. But when the first draft of a paper was presented by the director of Church and Society to the in-house Staff Executive in Geneva, the reaction was so hostile that it had to be withdrawn. Some members said that AIDS was essentially no different from other sexually transmitted diseases, such as herpes, others that it was a disease of choice. A member of the Communications Department became so tongue-tied at the prospect of even mentioning the word 'homosexual', that he said 'heterosexual' instead!

The General Secretary raised the issue in his opening remarks at the Zaire Executive, and it was agreed that the three sub-units on Church and Society, Education and the Christian Medical Commission would undertake a joint consultation as soon as possible. The consultation took place in June 1986 at Cartigny in Switzerland and was attended by eminent international medical experts, including Biel Kapita from Zaire and Courtney Bartholemew from Barbados, both of whom had just completed a WHO consultation on the same subject in Paris. Three continents were represented, and almost all the participants had been in close contact with the disease. Tom Tull, founder of the Parsonage in California, was HIV positive. There were two Roman Catholic participants: James McManus, who had worked with HIV drug abusers in Scotland, and Kevin Gordon, a distinguished theologian and ethicist from New York, who has since died.

In his opening address the General Secretary challenged the view that AIDS is in any sense a punishment from God:

AIDS is a disease and should be treated as such. God, who loves all human beings, cares for the wellbeing and health of every one of his children, and does not inflict any disease as a punishment.

The final consultation statement, which emerged from a painful and often deeply emotive encounter between conflicting 'evangelical' and 'liberal' viewpoints, called upon the Church to be the healing community. It must express its solidarity with people with AIDS through pastoral and social care and the protection of their rights, and should cooperate with other groups in educating the public in preventing transmission of the disease.

In the mysteries of life and death we encounter God; this encounter calls forth trust, hope and awe rather than paralysis and immobilisation. Those we cannot cure we can support and sustain in solidarity: 'I was hungry . . . thirsty . . . a stranger . . . naked . . . sick . . . imprisoned, and you fed . . . clothed . . . took care . . . visited me' (Matt. 25).

The AIDS crisis challenges us profoundly to be the Church in deed and in truth: *to be the Church as a healing community*. AIDS is heartbreaking and challenges the churches to break their own hearts, to repent of inactivity and of rigid moral attitudes. Since AIDS cuts across race, class, gender, age, sexual orientation and sexual expression, it challenges our fears and exclusions. The healing community itself will need to be healed by the forgiveness of Christ . . .

Since AIDS is a global epidemic, effective action by churches and individual Christians must extend not only to the AIDS neighbour closest at hand, but also through effective global collaboration to the stranger on the farthest side of the world.[34]

The Church and Society Working Committee reviewed the document at its Potsdam meeting and passed it to the WCC Executive, which at its Reykjavik meeting in September 1986 expressed warm appreciation for the work of the consultation.

The January 1987 meeting of the WCC Central Committee passed a recommendation urging the churches 'to make known the seriousness of the problem of AIDS and to take every opportunity to cooperate with one another and with medical, social and educational agencies and the mass media in appropriate educational programmes'. But in spite of a unanimous vote in its favour preceded by a powerful plea from Kevin Gordon that the Committee reject a 'narrow tit-for-tat God who sends AIDS as an act of divine retribution', none of the WCC's official communications channels made any reference at that time to the vote.

Church and Society also organised a public hearing during the 1987 Central Committee at which Jonathan Mann, director of WHO's AIDS Programme, Edmund Browning, Presiding Bishop of the US Episcopalian Church, and Bena-Silu, a scientist and member of the WCC Executive from Zaire, made presentations. Summing up the discussion, moderator John Habgood urged those present to encourage their churches to take a lead in making accurate information about AIDS available to their members, and offered the following reflection on the vulnerability of all human relationships:

The AIDS virus is fragile. For its transmission it depends upon intimate contact. And there is an interesting connection between intimacy and vulnerability. Every intimate contact makes us vulnerable in all sorts of ways not only through transmission of infection but also psychologically and in our personal identity. And this is why every civilization has in

34 *AIDS and the Church*, Church and Society Documents, No. 1, March 1987, p. 2.

various ways surrounded intimate relationships with rules, with structures, with ceremonies, with taboos. These have as it were protected the relationships. And what I see the AIDS epidemic as teaching us is that we cannot lightly treat these intimate relationships any longer. And that is where the world has lost its sense that close contact between human beings needs to be within an ordered framework. Then it is sure to recover that perspective. And this it seems to me is a moral and theological understanding which can be expressed in ways which are accessible not only to those with Christian commitment but to all those who think seriously about our human nature and our contacts with one another. I leave that there as a final theological reflection.[35]

Opposition to the sub-unit's advocacy of education for prevention came mainly from North American conservatives, the Romanian Orthodox and sections of the WCC Geneva staff, and there were some hostile press reactions. According to the *EIR Journal*, a La Rouche publication with headquarters in California, Church and Society's work was closely linked with plans for euthanasia in the Netherlands and population control in Thailand:

> Church and Society AIDS director . . ., a member of the Church of England who is closely linked to a gnostic faction within the Church's hierarchy, is a strong supporter of the hospice die-with-dignity approach to AIDS . . . Privately he has circulated a proposal in support of Thai 'condom king', Mechai Viravaidya, who has been praised by Britain's malthusian Prince Philip, president of the World Wildlife Fund, for having devised innovative coloured condoms for Third World populations, which can be an incentive for reducing birth rates in India, Pakistan and other nations with non-white populations.[36]

But in spite of such bizarre attempts to discredit the sub-unit's work there were some warm tributes, of which one of the most eloquent – and, as it turned out, ironically prophetic – came from R. P. Bernard, the epidemiologist who lost his job in a celebrated though also tragic incident at the Swiss ski resort of Zermatt where he had maintained, against the wishes of the local mayor, that the town's water supply was polluted. He wrote as follows:

> Esteemed General Secretary,
>
> In reading carefully *AIDS and the Church* by Church and Society I have come to admire the courage and frankness of the

35 John Habgood, *Ibid*, p. 19.
36 *EIR Journal*, La Rouche, California, October 2, 1987, p. 33.

46

mixed working group of the WHO, and Protestant and Catholic Churches representatives, in trying to evolve a consensus for the churches' guidance and leadership to combat and cope with AIDS, especially in its moral and social dimensions.

Kevin Gordon's closing sentence in the Central Committee summing up on AIDS should be pondered by all churches; 'AIDS may in the long run judge the churches' is the key statement in the 1987 Central Committee debate.

I am convinced now with Kevin Gordon that this challenge is the acid test for all churches at the end of the second millenium after Jesus Christ. *Oikoumene* now assumes new dimensions and not much time remains to achieve a painful consensus.

R. P. Bernard
(Translated from the French)

4 Creation at the Centre

We saw in chapter two that the integrity of creation is primarily about relationships – with God, within a community of being and between thought and action. In this chapter we shall examine the implications of this interpretation for our understanding of particular issues.

In the last three chapters we have seen how concern about the environment has been perceived in different parts of the world, and how Christians and others have responded from within their various traditions. We stressed the regional dimensions of these responses partly because it is at this level that the most fertile solutions seem possible, and partly to counter the all-pervasive idea in ecumenical circles that there has to be a monolithic 'global' view of everything.

In the process of summarising regional responses to environmental problems we concentrated on traditional cultural and religious views about creation – Mugambi's powers perceived in the environment, for example. This was a perfectly legitimate way to proceed because concern for the environment is the most recent item on the ecumenical agenda, and doctrines of creation express the way religions talk about it.

But it must be stressed that although doctrines of creation are important, what we are really concerned about is not primarily their rediscovery, but the restructuring of our entire framework of thought so that creation becomes foundational. This is what the integrity of creation is all about, and as we suggested in chapter two, it is only when we understand it in this way that it can truly serve as a basis for justice and peace.

To illustrate further this important point let us reconsider Gabriel Setiloane's comparison in chapter two, section (vi), between panentheism – the view that God works in and through the world – which he attributes to John Robinson, and African animism 'understood from inside by a very religious people'. Panentheism is one of several ways of characterising the relationship between God and the world, the others being pantheism, the view that they are one and the same (as advocated by Alister Hardy and some Asian religions), deism, which supposes that God made nature and then left it (save for occasional interventions) and traditional theism, which holds together, paradoxically, God's transcendence and immanence.

Setiloane is saying that with the exception of distinguished biologists like Hardy, western thought has so devalued nature that theology could not progress until Robinson and others began to question the entire basis of our understanding of God's relationship with the world, bringing it into line with what religious Africans have always known.

From an entirely different direction much the same point was made by John B. Cobb at the Annecy consultation on theocentric ethics (see Table I). Beginning by defining theology as 'self-conscious Christian reflection about important matters', Cobb lists some important theologies which have recently come into view:

We have had theologies of liberation, of women's experience, of Judaism, of culture, of religion, of the body, of worship, of humour, of play, of work, of institutions, of the church, of the world . . . Now we are adding one of nature. We cannot understand the church's response to a theology of nature apart from this multiplication of 'theologies of'. What is going on in this new language?

One way of understanding this language would be to suppose that this is simply a new way of speaking of 'doctrines of'. We could understand a theology of liberation as a doctrine of liberation, namely, as what the church teaches about liberation. Similarly we could understand a theology of women's experience as what the church teaches about women's experience. But to say this is to make immediately evident its inadequacy to what these theologies have been about. A theology of liberation is not asking what the church has said and now should say about liberation. It is arguing that all that the church says about all topics should be rethought from the perspective of the centrality to its mission of the liberation of the oppressed. It is a proposal about how to do *all* theology.[37]

Cobb welcomes these new theologies but criticises them for not listening sufficiently to one another. But now they are all increasingly being contained by more moderate theologies so that, in short, 'there is danger that liberation theology will become a doctrine of liberation in a general theology that is not itself liberated'.[38] He believes that advocates of the theology of nature have an important role to play now in bringing together representatives of all other theologies. In addition to providing a forum for them to listen more carefully to one another, theologians of nature can also help the others to lose their anthropocentrism by speaking on behalf of non-human creation, especially animals:

Animals can . . . be represented by human beings who have devoted themselves to studying how animals suffer at human hands and how Christian teaching has supported and encouraged

37 John B. Cobb, 'The Role of Theology of Nature in the Church', in Birch, Eakin and McDaniel, eds., *Liberating Life*, Orbis Books, 1990, p. 263.
38 *Ibid.*, p. 265.

their torture. This is a voice that no other 'theology of' will introduce.[39]

The theology of nature has an additional advantage in initiating such dialogue in that of all the various theologies it is ultimately the most inclusive.

The latter part of Cobb's presentation was concerned with Whitehead's philosophy, which we shall comment on later. But his Annecy paper as a whole was a plea for a recognition of the foundational character of creation/integrity of creation, or 'theocentric ethics', to use the phrase which ultimately came out of the deliberations of successive Church and Society Working Committees, and was also reflected in the Granvöllen JPIC meeting.

(i) Work ethics

In this and succeeding sections we shall consider a number of important ecumenical issues in the light of this new understanding of creation.

The need to rethink the Protestant Work Ethic – the view that an individual's social and religious worth is defined by their job – was strongly expressed at regional consultations in Glasgow and Manila (see Table I). During the former, predominantly young unemployed people, more women than men, described how their self-esteem was constantly undermined by the attitudes of employers, local officials, parents and even churches. An Irish participant pointed out that both the IRA and Protestant paramilitary groups capitalise on the fact that some unemployed school leavers will embrace violence as an alternative rite of passage to adulthood in place of their first paid job.

But lack of worth through unemployment was only one of several factors which Glasgow consultation participants were inhibited by. The following extract from their final report makes this clear and also suggests how the work ethic might be redefined in line with the view that people are not individual cogs in an industrial machine, but men and women living in community:

Attitudes towards women who stay at home to care for their children and families are revealing. This is not paid work, and so is not accorded the status which would be given to workers in paid employment carrying a similar responsibility . . . Our present system of values undervalues the work of women and of others in the caring professions. Qualities such as openness, cooperation, and compassion are not compatible with the

39 Ibid., p. 267.

'masculine' work ethic which currently prevails. The present system of values gives credence and reward to competition, aggression, and oppression, and discourages the expression of less assertive characteristics. This is emotionally damaging to men and women alike, creating a prison in which all are to some extent confined. The key to our emotional freedom lies in a shift of values such that men and women recognize the fundamental importance of the ability to care for and share with others.

'Work' could then become that contribution made by an individual for the maintenance, support or enrichment of the life of the community. Wealth-creating employment on the international, national and local basis would obviously still be crucial, and qualities of competition and assertiveness would continue to play a part. But all would recognize the limitations in terms of personnel requirements for this aspect of our economy, and the equal value of the contributions of the majority not within this sector. Education and training will necessarily play a crucial part in achieving these goals.[40]

The substitution of 'men and women in community' for people seen as individual cogs in a commercial machine is therefore likely to result in more justice, especially for women, and peace, in that less competition means less division.

But what we are really advocating here is a much more radical transformation whereby worth defined on the basis of economically productive activity is replaced by worth in accordance with our God-given understanding of who we are – men and women who, when able to establish relationships with one another, display a remarkable capacity for creativity and cooperation. This is what integrity of creation means here at its deepest level; once we understand and act upon it, justice and peace become almost axiomatic.

It is more difficult to apply these ideas to the Southeast Asian participants at the Manila consultation. In chapter two, section (iv), we saw the seductive arguments used by multinationals to justify the employment of women in the microelectronics industry: they are 'docile, easily manageable, able to sit for long hours', etc. Is this merely a recognition of the way these women are and what they are good at, or do other factors need to be acknowledged?

The Southeast Asian participants were even more insistent than the Scottish ones that the Protestant Work Ethic is harmful – more damaging

40 Howard Davis and David Gosling, eds., *Will the Future Work?*, WCC, Geneva, 1986, p. 112.

in developing than developed countries. Among reasons given were the speed and direction of the technology, the concentration of information and therefore power in the hands of a few, urban migration and the lack of proper legislation relating to the pay, health and rights of workers. Whatever the natural disposition of Malaysian women workers may be, the fact remains that they are underpaid, overworked and unprotected by custom, legislation, unions or anything else.

The Manila consultation branded the Protestant Work Ethic as 'competitive, divisive and an instrument of exploitation'. In its place participants wanted an ethic which reflects the Asian view of work as 'a duty or responsibility to maintain harmonious relationships in society'.[41] These sentiments may reflect Confucianism, with its emphasis on reciprocal relationships, but otherwise they are very similar to those of the Manila participants' Scottish counterparts except for the element of exploitation which the former associated with the involuntary migration of workers to the cities from once self-reliant rural communities.

The Scottish situation is by no means free from exploitation, but as Theodor Leuenberger, professor of economic history at the University of St Gallen, pointed out, European nations can soften the impact of unemployment by combining regional policy coordination (such as is likely to be possible in United Europe) with alternative types of economic activity (such as people working with computers from home). Similar policies could in theory be introduced in Southeast Asia, but this is unlikely to happen as long as multinationals want cheap labour and governments are willing to displace people from their land so that plantations suitable for the growth of cash crops for export can be developed.

There are additional elements of exploitation with regard to the situation of microelectronics in developing countries, and these are likely to become more acute as western industrial societies move towards the information society (i.e. the convergence of computing and telecommunications). We shall say more about this in the next chapter.

In his keynote address to the Manila consultation, Cardinal Sin indicated some of the ways in which the Roman Catholic Church is currently rethinking its theology of work. The papal encyclical *Laborem Exercens* defines workers as people who by their labour reflect and share God's creativity. By 'labour' is meant not just industrial and commercial labour – paid jobs – but agricultural, scientific, professional and intellectual work as well. All members of society are co-creators with God in the building up of society and deserve to be justly remunerated.

41 Feliciano Carino and David Gosling, eds., *Technology from the Underside*, NCCP, 1986, p. 95.

The encyclical proceeds to explain what is meant by the Genesis commands to 'subdue the earth' and to exercise 'dominion over the earth'. Cardinal Sin explained these as follows:

A proper interpretation of this text will need to take into account that this Biblical command was addressed to a farming people. Thus it can be interpreted as a challenge to cultivate the earth fruitfully and to be careful stewards of nature's limited riches. Farmers of all ages have had an instinctive sense not to violate nature, not to lay waste its resources. It was only the advent of profit-hungry entrepreneurs of the industrial age that brought about the destruction of nature.[42]

Elsewhere the encyclical reverses the view implicit in the Protestant Work Ethic that labour must serve capital:

Briefly stated *Laborem Exercens* views justice as meaning that capital is made to serve labour. Faced with the conflict between the capitalist owners of the means of production and the mass of the people who share in the process of production solely by their labour, the Pope argues for solidarity with the struggle of the workers, and for justice, where labourers have access to the wealth of society and are guaranteed a living wage and participation in decision making. In a statement that causes anxiety amongst capitalist entrepreneurs, the Pope stated that 'in order to achieve social justice . . . there is need for ever new movements of solidarity among the workers and with the workers'.[43]

We have said nothing in this section about workers' physical environment. But we have affirmed creation as foundational or 'at the centre'. This has been done by asserting that any new Christian work ethic must be based not on individual 'worth' according to a paid job, but rather on the interaction of people within and beyond their community. Their physical context is, of course, important, and in the next section we shall explore this aspect further.

(ii) **Computers at the work place**

Around the mid-1980s the WCC computerised its Geneva headquarters. The results, initially at least, were chaotic. Administrative staff scrambled up and down corridors at the beck and call of printers and in pursuit of transferred phone calls. Senior executives were unexpectedly bleeped out

42 Jaime Cardinal Sin, 'Towards an Environmentally Sensitive Christian Work Ethic', in Carino and Gosling, *Ibid.*, p. 5.
43 *Ibid.*, p. 5.

54

of chapel before the astonished eyes of visiting hierarchs. Everyone began to feel oppressed by the new technology.

The 'environment' created by computers at the work place was investigated by Göran Collste, lecturer in social ethics at the University of Uppsala, at the Glasgow consultation (see Table I) and in subsequent discussions. In addition to basing his arguments for a new work ethic on the needs of workers using computers, Collste looked at the question of how far any new technology can in itself be humane.

Collste's analysis begins by considering what kinds of theories can be used to evaluate technological change and employment policies. He opts for ethical theories which critique choices according to their consequences (i.e. teleological theories), and among these the ones which maximise usefulness (i.e. utilitarian theories). Usefulness is related to the satisfaction of basic human need, which is defined as something which (i) will cause suffering if denied, (ii) is generally prevalent in all men and women, and (iii) is relatively constant over time.

The detailed elaboration of basic needs is a matter for the human sciences. It will, however, include physical requirements such as food, air, space, etc. and social needs, such as a sense of community, self-realisation (using and developing one's innate resources and gifts), a measure of autonomy and some participation in decision-making.

Applying this theory to computerisation in Swedish industry, Collste concludes that while possibilities for gratifying material demands have increased, those for gratifying psychological and social needs have diminished. Some workers have achieved greater self-realisation, while others require fewer skills for work, leading to polarisation. The sense of work community has declined, some individual workers have experienced considerable isolation, and management has achieved greater and greater power to direct and control the work process.

Thus, in Sweden at any rate, the introduction of computers has been detrimental to the achievement of a new work ethic. But things could have turned out differently had there been more consultation at the outset between management and unions. Collste concludes:

> The question then arises: who should be responsible for controlling the direction of new technology? From a Swedish viewpoint, with its corporatist structures and powerful labour organization, it is natural to answer 'the trade unions'. However, it is a hard task to control the introduction of new technology when computer systems, for the most part, are imported and give little room for modification and alternative designs. This fact has stimulated efforts to design new computer systems in cooperation with the workers who will use them. The starting point is to determine what the workers themselves require and then design

systems on the basis of these requirements. This is a path which will have to be followed – and should be followed – if in contrast to so much past technology, it is to promote the wellbeing of those who use it. A new 'work ethic', therefore, is not just about changing values and attitudes which are no longer appropriate to an age of computing and highly automated systems – it is a practical step towards achieving a more humane technology and a more responsible society because of a more involved work-force.[44]

Collste's new work ethic endorses our earlier view of 'men and women in community' as foundational, extending it to take into account the fact that they also live in an environment shaped by technology. All of this together is his 'theology of creation', in Cobb's sense. But although Collste would agree that 'men and women in community and in relationship with their physical environment' is foundational, he would see no reason to regard this as a theological statement.

Some members of the Potsdam Working Committee were unhappy about Collste's analysis because it was not presented in theological terms. Others, however, considered this an advantage because they thought that it was more likely to enable Christians and secular ethicists to work together, as for example, in the setting up of new legislation for United Europe.

Deontological ethical theories (i.e. views of morality based on duty or the essential rightness of certain acts) are often considered to be more theologically based than teleological ones which emphasise the consequences of choices. But there is no valid reason for such a conclusion, and in section (iv) we shall see how modern biological knowledge can undercut deontological theories whose principles have no basis in scientific fact.

(iii) Relating science and religion

The assumption underlying the Protestant Work Ethic that people at work are individuals whose worth is determined by a set of external factors is paralleled by fallacies about the way science and technology operate.

The tendency to view living organisms as machines has not only been damaging to the biological sciences, but has caused difficulties for our understanding of the relationship between God, humanity and nature. Our revised view of science, which we shall call an ecological model, is much more amenable to the theological affirmation of the centrality of creation than the mechanistic model which it largely replaces.

44 Göran Collste, 'Towards a Normative Work Ethic', in Davis and Gosling, *Op. cit.* (4), p. 99.

The ecological view of science is advocated by Charles Birch, formerly professor of zoology in the University of Sydney, and recipient of the 1990 Templeton Prize for progress in science and religion. Birch identifies the tendency in physics, chemistry and biology to treat all atoms, cells and living organisms, including people, as machines. Machines relate externally to other machines and are subject only to the laws of mechanics.

Birch concedes that this mechanistic methodology of science has had great success. Newton's laws got us to the moon, and the advances of molecular biology are also triumphs for this approach. However 'it is one thing to investigate entities such as living organisms as if they were machines (methodological mechanism); it is quite another to insist that these entities *are* machines (metaphysical mechanism)'.[45]

According to this mechanistic (or substantialist) view of the universe, 'God the prime mover becomes the occasional mechanic returning to tune the mechanism'.[46] Such an interventionist view of God is deism, which we met in chapter three when dealing with the response of North American fundamentalists to AIDS. We have also contrasted the deist heresy with panentheism, which affirms God's continuous creative activity at all times and in all places.

Birch's account of the relationships between God, humanity and nature is derived from the ecological view that organisms can only be understood in relation to their total environment, and that internal relationships are at least as important as external ones. He appeals to David Bohm's 'implicate order' for support from the world of physics, and uses arguments from Whitehead to present a God who is consistent, loving and in some senses personal:

> I am asked whether the ecological God is personal. This is a question we must face. However, we need to be careful in using the word person. The image of person is bound up with the substantialist idea of a person as self-contained. It is not a biblical word. It came into theology with the doctrine of the Trinity which tried to put together ideas about God, the world and people. But in the sense that God is involved in my personal being and in yours and all of us are involved in God's being, God is personal, very much so.[47]

45 Charles Birch, 'Values, Responsibilities and Commitments', in David Gosling and Bert Musschenga, eds., *Science Education and Ethical Values*, WCC, Geneva and Georgetown University Press, Washington, D.C., 1985, p. 22.
46 *Ibid.*, p. 23.
47 *Ibid.*, p. 29.

Birch's views about the personhood of God are similar to those of a BCC Study Report, *The Forgotten Trinity*.[48] These were first discussed at the Amsterdam consultation on 'Science Education and Ethics', which proposed new teaching models incorporating socio-ethical goals into science from the start. The Amsterdam consultation noted the damage done when mechanistic models of science are exported to developing countries:

> Developing countries have become increasingly aware of the need for western science and technology as a means to progress and enhancement of economic and political wellbeing. The mechanistic world-view implicit in science is usually incompatible with the traditional systems of the developing countries where life is perceived as a whole. In the transfer of science and technology to third world countries an awareness of the depersonalising effect of western science would facilitate assessment of the types of technology that are best suited for implementation.[49]

We saw some examples of the integrated world-views of developing countries in chapter two.

Mechanistic assumptions about the universe are not only being challenged by the biological sciences. During the Bossey consultation on 'Science and the Theology of Creation', John Polkinghorne, President of Queens' College, Cambridge and a former professor of theoretical physics, referred to the totally non-mechanistic openness which underlies all natural processes:

> The world is no mere mechanism. It has a flexibility, a suppleness within its processes, a freedom for the whole universe to be itself, a freedom for us to act within that universe of which we are part. God has not only given freedom to the whole world and to humankind but also has reserved some freedom within the subtleness of process for its own action.[50]

Arguing from the behaviour of matter, Polkinghorne rejects both mechanical and organic models of the universe in preference for 'something in between'. Openness and new emergent properties of the

---

48 *The Forgotten Trinity*, 1 The Report of the BCC Study Commission on Trinitarian Doctrine Today, BCC 1989; 2 A Study Guide on issues contained in the Report, BCC 1989; 3 A Selection of Papers presented to the BCC Study Commission BCC/CCBI 1991.

49 *Ibid.*, p. 104.

50 John Polkinghorne, 'The Unity of Truth in Science and Theology' in *Science and the Theology of Creation*, Church and Society Documents, No. 4, August 1988, p. 31.

universe are caused by the interplay of chance and necessity in the realisation 'of a vision which is discovered only through its own realisation'.

The fact that openness exists within the universe's creative processes means that the future in that sense is open:

> God does not know the future because the future is not there to be known . . . I think that involved in creation was not only a kenosis of God's omnipotence, but also a kenosis of God's omniscience. God knows all that can be known, but the future cannot be known. If that is right, then we will have to incorporate within theology scope for a temporal pole in God as well as an eternal pole. Not necessarily in the way that the process theologians do.[51]

Polkinghorne's disclaimer with regard to process theology marks an important distinction between his ideas (and those of Keith Ward, who has also suggested the possibility of a di-polar God) and those of Birch and Cobb, who base their views largely on Whitehead's process philosophy. Process theologians believe that every entity is relational in its most fundamental nature and is constituted by its relations. This accords well with the findings of the biological and human sciences, but most physicists, including Polkinghorne, are not convinced that the ecological model is compatible with the fundamental physics of relativity and quantum theory.

In the context of correspondence with John Polkinghorne about the possibility of a Hippocratic oath for scientists, Wolfhart Pannenberg, professor of systematic theology in the University of Munich, stressed the urgent need for scientists and theologians to engage in mutual dialogue as follows:

> In contrast to many theologians, especially Karl Barth and his school, I am of the opinion that such a dialogue is necessary for the sake of theology, if God is to be affirmed as the creator of the world we actually experience.[52]

Thus whether we consider the dialogue between science and theology from the point of view of the biological or the physical sciences, we encounter a relationship between creator and creation which is more intimate, constant, and open than was possible according to the mechanistic model of the universe. In the process of moving in the direction of Birch's interiorised organic relationships or Polkinghorne's 'freedom for the whole universe to be itself', we have not only substituted

---

51 *Ibid.*, p. 31.
52 Wolfhart Pannenberg, letter to John Polkinghorne, 6 September 1988.

better models, but we have located creation in its rightful place at the centre of theological belief and action.

(iv) Co-creators or co-workers?

When does life begin? The openness which physicists detect at the heart of the universe's creative processes is paralleled by an indeterminacy in the biological sciences about the stage in the process of increasing biological complexity at which we can say that life begins. The answer to our question, essentially, is that just as in everyday experience there is no exact moment at which, say, dawn breaks, so, as we move from the fertilisation of an egg to what is known as the primitive streak stage approximately two weeks later, there is no 'moment' at which we can say that life has begun. We know that dawn has broken, we know that we are encountering life; we cannot give a precise moment for either, nor shall we ever be able to do so.

This topic was the subject of a lively discussion with Russian Orthodox scientists and theologians at the Tambov Working Committee. The stages of the discussion were, first, to decide what in the context of biotechnology we mean by justice, peace and the integrity of creation; secondly, to ask to what extent are we willing to live with uncertainties with regard to the results of biotechnological research on the grounds that we are co-creating an open future with God?

There was a consensus among representatives of various theological traditions that justice in relation to biotechnology should be understood in economic terms. The fact that seeds of herbicide-resistant crop plants and the herbicides to which they are resistant must often be purchased from the same multinationals via sub-companies making exploitation easy, was given as an example of potential injustice.

Peace was exemplified as the use of genetically engineered crop plants to increase yields of food to feed the hungry.

The integrity of creation was taken to mean increasing our understanding of the way life processes work, their underlying biological sameness, and the essential continuity from egg and sperm through the moment of fertilisation to the primitive streak stage when differentiation begins. Some participants argued that cells possess 'potentiality', but most were not in agreement. The Russian scientists present, some of whom were Academy Marxists and therefore officially atheists, maintained that there are more similarities than differences between human and non-human life. They argued that other primates are barely distinct from humans at a biological level, and that although self-awareness may mark the distinction, it is more an emergent than an intrinsic property. Understood in this way, integrity of creation was accepted as foundational to subsequent discussion.

The question was asked: when we do research do we co-participate with God in a future already known by God in which our position and role are predetermined, or are we part of a process of co-creating an open future with God? Most Orthodox found the second option difficult. We may use natural science, they argued, to 'dust the icon of God's image in nature' so as to understand God's character more clearly, but to claim, with John Polkinghorne, that science reveals a universe which points in the direction of an emerging openness, was unacceptable.

At this point in the discussion, Jay McDaniel, professor of theology at Hendrix Methodist College in the USA, suggested that animals and non-human creation in general assist human beings in the task of co-creation. Taking up Birch's view that all things possess intrinsic value according to their degree of sentience, McDaniel argued for a gradation of co-creative function based on the same criteria. But Bishop Feofan, a Russian Orthodox member of the Church and Society Committee, insisted that human beings can never be more than co-workers with God, and that we only enjoy that status by virtue of (i) our being the crown of creation, and (ii) the fact that we are called to freedom (which we do not yet possess), a calling which is not shared by non-human life.

According to Russian Orthodoxy it is freedom, not reason, which establishes us as the crown of creation, and our freedom can be increased by religious practices and a life of asceticism to develop potentialities which we possess, but the rest of creation does not. Creation will ultimately be redeemed (or transfigured, to use the evocative Orthodox term), but only through us.

Some Orthodox present suggested a hierarchy within creation; others maintained that the notion of a 'differentiated unity' could provide a good definition of the integrity of creation. It would satisfy animal behaviourists who argue that the capacity to transcend both nurture and nature (i.e. to exercise freedom) is shown by some non-human species. Reference was made to St Maximus the Confessor, who believed this to be the case, but only via the intermediacy of humans.

The major differences between Russian Orthodoxy and the other main views represented in Tambov may be summarised as follows:

	Orthodox	Other Main Views
God	Future ordained (God knows it). Calls only humans into freedom.	Future open (God does not know it). God works alongside and with all creation.
Humanity	Humans alone act in accord with or violate natural order.	Humans co-create the future with God.
Nature	All non-human species are subject to the set order created by God.	All species co-create the future but in accordance with a 'differentiated unity'.

We have summarised this discussion carefully because it illustrates some of the difficult (but also often exciting) issues which arise when questions concerning the relationship between science and theology are looked at from the perspective of more than one theological tradition.

Biotechnology featured in the WCC statement for World Environment Day in 1987, and at the 1988 Hanover Central Committee, at which Mary Seller, reader in developmental genetics at Guy's Hospital, presented a convincing case in favour of the continuation of experiments in biotechnology – the application of molecular biology to the diagnosis of genetic diseases, for example. Her views were opposed by some German delegates, who referred to experiments conducted by the Nazis, and some Third World members who were opposed to anything to do with science. But her arguments were endorsed by the majority.

(v) Cancelling the debts

In chapter two, section (iii), we saw how the debts that developing countries such as Brazil owe to the international banks are instrumental in forcing people to leave their inherited land to live in cities or work for poor wages on plantations from which cash crops are exported to pay off the debts. We also saw how this issue relates to the large-scale destruction of forests with loss of irreplaceable species and aggravation of the global problem of the absorption of greenhouse gases.

In this section we shall consider the thinking underlying the statement of the Council of Churches for Britain and Ireland to the Earth Summit in Rio de Janeiro (see Appendix), and in particular why attempts to equate Christianity solely with 'green' environmental policies are felt to be inadequate. But first we must understand how crippling debts by developing countries to the commercial banks, the World Bank and the International Monetary Fund (IMF) have come about. We shall then argue, from the standpoint of our affirmation of the integrity of creation as the basis for justice and peace, that insofar as all creation – forests, land, the oceans – has intrinsic value, damage done to it by industrial nations during the last half century must now be given a retrospective price tag. If this is done, then a strong moral argument exists to cancel many of the debts which developing countries have built up during approximately the same half century and which are currently aggravating all their problems in relation to justice, peace and the state of the environment. These debts currently total more than US $1500 billion and are increasing by US $7.5 billion every month.

At the end of the Second World War the World Bank, the IMF and the international tariff body (GATT) were set up to fix terms of international lending and borrowing and the price of goods. Many developing countries embarked on a process of industrialisation modelled on the West which set in motion migrations from countryside to city producing vast urban conurbations as in Manila, São Paulo, Lagos and elsewhere.

The industrial North exploited cheap Third World labour, cheap resources (e.g. wood and minerals) and polluted the environment at no cost whatsoever. This pollution during the period under consideration – from the mid-forties until now – did not only occur in developing countries; the USA poisoned all life in many Canadian lakes, Britain destroyed many Scandinavian trees, and vast tracts of Eastern Europe were polluted within and across borders by unregulated industry.

Whereas the USA's Marshall Aid Plan gave large sums of money to Western Europe to rebuild its shattered cities with no expectation of any return other than prospects for satisfactory future trading – which turned out to be a splendid investment – IMF and World Bank loans and loans by the commercial banks have had to be paid back with interest. The 1973/74 oil crisis aggravated First/Third World imbalances because it meant that Third World industrialisation cost more to fuel on account of oil price increases, and essential imported goods from the industrial countries cost more because everything cost more to produce.

Since loans could only be repaid in 'strong' currencies, developing countries were increasingly only able to repay them, as we have seen, by growing cash crops for export to the industrial North. This involved the cultivation of large tracts of land which could often only be made available by destroying forests. And since people do not willingly surrender their inherited land, the most 'successful' governments were those who knew how to suppress the rights of their own people, especially military dictatorships which could also be counted on to purchase arms, partly to keep their own people in check, and partly to perpetuate quarrels with their neighbours, thus enhancing their reputation for 'machismo'.

We see, therefore, that during a period in which the industrial North prospered in accordance with economic principles which paid no attention to environmental damage, developing countries which had borrowed money to move their own economies in the direction of self-sufficiency were plunged increasingly into a situation in which (i) people actually growing food on plantations were hungry, (ii) fertilisers purchased at exorbitant prices to increase food yields exhausted and damaged the soil, and (iii) pesticides needed to protect new strains of crops harmed the soil, impaired the health of cultivators, and were produced in places like Bhopal where not too many questions were asked about safety.

The connections between justice, peace and the integrity of creation in such a situation are obvious. It will also be clear why the *cancellation* of the debts – not their forgiveness, as some organisations have recommended – is a top priority. Attention must be given to the question of which debts and which banks, because, as Charles Elliott points out, the international banking system and the role of commercial banks is very complex.[53] But the moral and theological argument for cancellation remains very strong, if only on account of the needs of people whose lives are threatened if the policies of financial donors are rigidly enforced – a point made by the Vatican's Justice and Peace Commission. There have been various refinements to the argument for cancellation of the debts, such as rescheduling them according to certain conditions. The Sofia meeting of the Church and Society Working Committee made a proposal to set up an international fund derived from a tax on fossil fuels to be paid to nations in proportion to the size of their areas of afforestation. Most of this money would go to developing countries, and would be seen as payment for keeping carbon locked up in trees. Receiver nations would not be constrained in the use to which the money was put, but they would have a strong financial incentive to retain forests and plant more of them.

But the main thrust of our argument is that the theological attribution of intrinsic value to all creation means that the environmental damage of the last forty years must now retrospectively be given a price tag, and that the whole basis of reductionist economics whereby – as Lesslie Newbigin has pointed out – economics is separated from ethics and justice to become 'the science of the working of the market as a self-operating mechanism modelled on the Newtonian universe' – must be challenged.[54]

If this can be accomplished, then much would have been achieved to reduce some of the world's worst poverty, many of the forces currently destroying vast areas of the globe would have been weakened, and the divisions and tensions which keep many military arsenals full would disappear.

(vi) **Theocentric ethics**

In the last few sections we have demonstrated in various ways how our understanding of the integrity of creation as foundational can influence our perspective of a number of important issues. In this and the concluding section we shall highlight some of the stages whereby this understanding was reached, firstly in terms of the annual Working Committee meetings of Church and Society (which reached a consensus about what was

---

53 Charles Elliott, 'The Ethics of International Debt', in *Finance and Ethics*, Occasional Paper No. 11, Centre for Theology and Public Issues, University of Edinburgh, 1987, p. 27.
54 Lesslie Newbigin, *Foolishness to the Greeks*, SPCK, 1986, p. 30.

64

described as 'theocentric ethics'), then via the Council-wide JPIC process and the Seoul JPIC World Congress in March 1990.

The first meeting of the post-Vancouver Church and Society Working Committee proposed the following set of relationships between theology, ethics, scientific and social analysis and action:

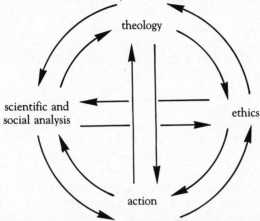

Careful scientific analysis (i.e. the use of data supplied by experts) had been an important feature of Church and Society's work for many years, whereas social analysis received little prominence until Wolfhart Pannenberg called for more of it at a joint meeting with Faith and Order in 1984. The programme subsequently relied heavily on case studies carried out by Working Committee members in their home areas, and evaluation of them was carried out with the assistance of two new members, both professors of sociology – T. K. Oommen from India, and Mady Laeyendecker-Thung from the Netherlands.

The 'Bossey circle', as it became known, represented a consensus by the twenty-five strong Working Committee – international, interdisciplinary and interconfessional – that any piece of work conducted by the sub-unit on behalf of the churches would incorporate all four elements.

It is illuminating to consider the interfaces between different elements around the circle. Some have been studied more than others. Thus scholars such as John Polkinghorne and Arthur Peacocke (both of whom participated in the programme) have explored the interface between theology and science. Robin Gill has studied the frontier between theology and social analysis, and it is interesting to note that he regards the social context of theology as being especially important in relation to creation.[55] But other interfaces in the diagram are more problematic, so

55 Robin Gill, 'Theology: A Social System. Models for a Systematic Theology', in the Scottish Journal of Theology, Vol. 42, p. 7.

that although we may refer to the circle from time to time, it will not be regarded as more than a useful methodological tool.

In August 1985 Faith and Order responded to a request of Church and Society by drawing up the document *The Integrity of Creation in the Light of the Apostolic Faith*. This suggested that biblical expressions such as new creation, covenant, wisdom and word of God and even kingdom of God may once have performed a conciliar function similar to JPIC or other ecumenical slogans. The document did not develop this theme, but it is interesting to make such comparisons between the 'middle axioms' or 'realisable utopias' of modern ecumenism and the 'slogans' of the early church. Thus we might ask: was 'new creation' the original doctrine of creation infused with Christian hope and the need for action?

This particular Faith and Order document was also unusual in that it stressed the role of liturgy in affirming the totality of creation:

> The liturgy is the appropriate place for the celebration of the joy of creation and for its sharing: thanksgiving for the harvest may underline our faith in our creating and caring God; the symbols of water and oil, bread and wine, incense and light refer to the gifts of nature and to their Giver as well; the old tradition of blessings and benedictions brings in the world of labour; liturgical acts of solidarity with the victims of violence and death on the occasion of funerals and symbolic public processions for justice and peace, all these are effective signs of Christian hope and faith in God's promise of the integrity of creation.[56]

The lack of prominence given to this document in subsequent discussions may stem from the reaction of Charles Birch from Church and Society's Working Committee, who rated it 'zero minus for an undergraduate essay'.[57]

Integrity of creation was the subject of a small consultation between Faith and Order and Church and Society held in York in May 1986, and it was while this was exploring phrases such as 'ambiguity in creation' that the Chernobyl accident occurred.

However, the most substantial joint venture taken by the two sub-units was a consultation on Creation and the Kingdom of God held in Dublin in May 1988. Scientific representatives from Church and Society took a long, hard look at Faith and Order's explication of the Creed, *Confessing One Faith*, and Faith and Order's theologians made an equally searching critique of Church and Society's documents.

56 *The Integrity of Creation in the Light of the Apostolic Faith*, Faith and Order Commission Meeting, Stavanger, August 1985, p. 8.
57 Charles Birch, letter to John Deschner, 6 November, 1985.

Church and Society's critique of *Confessing One Faith* registered serious doubts about theological statements which are no longer tenable from the point of view of modern science or philosophy – the notion of God as 'designer', for example:

> The use of the word 'design' suggests a metaphysical notion of the sort discarded by modern science. It would therefore be better to refer to the implicit order of creation which is illuminated by the behaviour and teaching of Jesus Christ, including his recognition of the natural world as an icon of proper relation to God's purpose.[58]

'Design', and also 'implicit order of creation' were subjected to an even sharper critique by John Polkinghorne at the Bossey consultation mentioned in section (iii). It is anticipated that this joint work will be continued by Faith and Order after their 1993 World Conference.

In 1986 the Church and Society Working Committee at Potsdam had begun to explore JPIC from a variety of theological and regional perspectives. Thus Heino Falcke, professor of theology from Erfurt in the former GDR, argued that although continuity exists between the Vancouver phrase 'integrity of creation' and the 'sustainable society' adopted at the 1974 Bucharest Conference, the change represents a major shift in emphasis away from anthropocentrism:

> Whereas in the phrase 'sustainable society' the ecological questions are related to society and its future, the phrase 'the integrity of creation' takes in the whole of creation and views society as part of this whole.[59]

The logic of such a shift in emphasis, Falcke argued, is that human beings, far from behaving according to the laws of natural selection, lording it over the rest of creation, must act according to the principle of ecological justice.

It was at the Potsdam meeting that Charles Birch described justice, peace and the integrity of creation as the 'three momentous instabilities of our time' and urged that the interconnections between them be explored. Reiterating his view that the mechanistic understanding of the world has contributed to the present environmental crises, Birch appealed for a new rapprochement between science and religion and also between economics and ecology.[60]

58 *Creation and the Kingdom of God*, Church and Society Documents No. 5, August 1988, p. 51.
59 Heino Falcke, 'The Integrity of Creation in the Current Ecumenical Debate', in the *Church and Society Working Committee Report*, Potsdam, July 1986, p. 54.
60 Charles Birch, *Ibid.*, p. 43, 44.

The sub-unit identified three priority areas for future work: (i) theological and ethical approaches to JPIC with respect to a theology of nature, a study of the value of life and a life-centred ethic, and a study of ecumenical social ethics which should begin with an examination of the ethical assumptions underlying all previous Church and Society work; (ii) regional case studies in the area of 'science, technology and the environment' (similar to the Manila consultation and Marshalls team visit); and (iii) responses to urgent social and environmental issues, such as nuclear safety, AIDS and biotechnology.

The third Working Committee in Glion in September 1987 combined theology of nature and the value of life and a life-centred ethic under the single heading 'theocentric ethics'. This was to serve as a basis for environmental ethics, justice and peace as follows:

A theocentric perspective towards nature holds together both poles of our understanding – the specifically human and the broader context of the whole natural world in which human life is set. A theocentric ethic tries to give value to both, avoiding on the one hand the mistake of seeing all value as human value, and on the other hand the mistake of failing to accept our human responsibility for much of the world's evil and our call to new life in Christ. God holds all aspects of creation together in interdependence and creative tension . . . We are in fact part of a community of life which forms a single interrelated whole, and in which subjects other than ourselves have their own intrinsic value. How far within the web of life this intrinsic value extends, and how different values are related to one another, are matters of much debate. A sound environmental ethic, however, needs some vision of this kind to sustain it if it is not to become transformed into yet another means of asserting the overriding importance of human interests. Unless there is respect for the freedom of all creatures to be themselves, there is unlikely to be respect for the freedom of all people to be themselves. Within the community of life freedom is indivisible. Here our consideration of the moral aspect of 'the integrity of creation' is clearly tied to the ideas of 'justice' and 'peace'. Liberation is to function at all levels of the created order. All three terms, 'justice', 'peace', and 'the integrity of creation' are to be recognized as indispensable dimensions of a contemporary Christian ethic. With this awareness, we can work to build a moral framework capable of providing significant and inclusive nurture for all of God's people and their fellows-in-creation.[61]

61 *Church and Society Working Committee Report*, Potsdam, July 1986, p. 41.

Thus integrity of creation becomes foundational to justice and peace, which was our contention at the beginning of this chapter and which we have illustrated from various standpoints.

The Glion meeting was distinguished by a detailed and exhaustive analysis of the ethical assumptions underlying all Church and Society's previous work by James Gustafson, then professor of Christian ethics in the University of Chicago. Gustafson divided types of moral discourse into four categories: *prophetic* (indictment and the setting out of ideal future states), *narrative* (sustaining the community memory with a dramatic story), *ethical* (the balancing of presumptions in order to decide what to do), and *policy* (determining what is desirable within the constraints of what is possible).[62]

The Marshalls team visit can be used to illustrate each of these four kinds of moral discourse. Nuclear tests in the Pacific have caused some ecumenical bodies to condemn the USA and pronounce God's judgement on it in the name of justice – this, in Gustafson's terminology, is a *prophetic* type of moral discourse, sometimes appropriate but usually counterproductive. The stories of people who have lost their island homes and suffered ill health because of the tests are *narrative* types of discourse – powerfully evocative, but impossible for governments and policy-makers to respond to, except via cash handouts, which may damage the interests of the wider community.

Ethical discourse balances the interests of fallout victims against those of poor people suffering malnutrition, unemployment and a sense of hopelessness, and recommends a way forward that will enable everybody to grow stronger by taking responsibility for their own lives. In this particular case it also recognises the need for justice between generations and right of access to past medical records in order to plan responsibly for future health needs. Finally, *policy* discourse addresses the US Congress with a request for information which is in its power to grant – access to medical records and the courts – and does so without an accompanying anti-US ideology.

Gustafson's analysis of WCC literature from about 1970 onwards concludes that prophetic statements have tended to obscure more reasoned social ethics, that policy recommendations have been conspicuous by their absence and that certain basic concepts such as justice have never been adequately explored by the WCC.

But although narrative discourse may not move the politicians and decision makers as much as policy statements, it often possesses a remarkable potential for triggering action among groups of people with

62 James Gustafson, *Ibid.*, p. 170.

similar experiences. Thus at the Manila consultation Darlene's televised account of her struggles with the legacy of militarism in the Marshalls was much more effective in rousing Filipino feelings against the Marcos régime than the final consultation pronouncements about injustice. Here Gustafson develops David Tracy's notion of the 'analogical imagination' to explain why such bilateral encounters are much more likely to trigger appropriate action than the time (and culture) honoured procedure of abstraction leading to generalised principles which are then projected back into new situations.[63] His argument suggests that what in ecumenical circles is often put forward as a 'global' perspective may have become so abstract as to be little more than a function of the process whereby such a viewpoint has been obtained.

The Just, Participatory and Sustainable Society (JPSS) which preceded JPIC has often been criticised from the point of view of its third element, sustainability, which some have felt to be modelled too closely on the 'limits to growth' arguments of the early 1970s. But as we have seen, the assumption of a single global society is also questionable, especially by people who experience the injustice, oppression and distorted values which are latent in so many of the international links in our modern world – technology, the media, economics and so on. On the other hand JPIC does not presuppose any such underlying global view, and is much more compatible with regional, cultural and other kinds of diversity.

(vii) **Global consensus?**

At the same time that Church and Society was studying specific issues within the broad JPIC framework, JPIC staff were organising cross-Council consultations in preparation for the World Convocation in Seoul in March 1990. Church and Society Working Committee members participated in these, especially the Granvöllen meeting on the Integrity of Creation in March 1988. This consultation was strongly influenced by native American and other indigenous peoples who believe that a deep respect for all creation must form the basis for our actions:

For the sake of all creation, theology must begin with creation. Just as concerned Christian people have begun to learn that true peace can only be realised through the establishment of justice and that peace flows naturally out of justice, so now we must begin to learn that justice and then peace flow naturally out of a deep respect for all creation. Thus for Indigenous Peoples a much more theologically sound expression would be 'CREATION, JUSTICE AND PEACE'.

63 *Ibid.*, p. 176.

70

The acceptance of this position by the consultation as a whole was an important landmark in the JPIC process.

Shortly after the Granvöllen consultation the WCC Executive, meeting in Istanbul, set out the purpose of the JPIC World Convocation as follows:

> The purpose of the World Convocation will be to make theological affirmations on justice, peace and the integrity of creation and to identify the major threats to life in these three areas and show their interconnectedness and make and propose to the churches acts of mutual commitment in response to them.

Preparatory regional JPIC conferences were held in the Pacific (September 1988), Europe (Basle, May 1989), Asia (September 1989), and Latin America (December 1989). Many of the findings referred to in previous chapters were fed into these.

Preparatory meetings for the Seoul Convocation were also held by groups of Orthodox theologians (Sofia 1987 and Minsk 1989), the Pontifical Council on Justice and Peace (Vatican 1989) and the World Alliance of Reformed Churches (Seoul 1989).[64] The Vatican turned down an invitation to co-sponsor the World Convocation, though Roman Catholic participants made a significant contribution.

The Convocation voted in favour of ten affirmations and a four-fold act of covenanting, as follows: all exercise of power is accountable to God; God's option for the poor; the equal value of all races and peoples; male and female are created in the image of God; truth is the foundation of a community of free people; peace belongs to Jesus Christ; creation is beloved of God; land belongs to God; dignity and commitment belong to the younger generation; and human rights are given by God. Participants covenanted to work for: a just economic order and liberation from bondage to foreign debt; the true security of all nations and people and for a culture of non-violence; preserving the gift of the earth's atmosphere and for building a culture that can live in harmony with creation's integrity; and an end to racism.

Important though these affirmations and covenants undoubtedly are, they do not completely fulfil the hopes and expectations for the Convocation as set out in Vancouver. But one wonders if any global conference could conceivably have done justice to an agenda incorporating so many points of view from different regions and confessions.

But perhaps global visions have had their day, and regional events which cross-fertilise one another are now the most viable way forward. We shall consider one such regional event, the Basle JPIC Ecumenical Assembly, in the next chapter.

---

64 Gennadios Limouris, *Justice, Peace and the Integrity of Creation: Insights from Orthodoxy*, WCC, Geneva, 1990.

71

5 From Basle to Britain

In his opening address to the 1988 Lambeth Conference, the then Archbishop of Canterbury, Robert Runcie, urged 'strong Anglican support for the World Conference on Peace, Justice and the Integrity of Creation', reminding delegates of the words of Barbara Ward to the previous Lambeth Conference: 'We have only one earth. Is it not worth our love?'

By and large British participation in the JPIC process has been minimal Of the 120 European organisations which displayed their activities in a workshop on the future of Europe at the Basle Assembly, only two were from Britain. And of the six hundred journalists who reported the same event, only four were British. According to John Yates, Bishop of Gloucester, who attended the Conference,

> For many British Christians, putting together Justice, Peace and (strange phrase) the Integrity of Creation is a novel idea, but there is much we can learn from it. Most of our European brothers and sisters have a more vivid impression than we have of the brokenness and disintegration of God's good and unified creation through war, injustice and (now) pollution. The Churches can offer a vision of the Creation restored through Christ to wholeness (integrity). That is a vision we need here in Britain too.

We shall now consider what took place at the Basle Assembly in some detail before describing JPIC initiatives currently taking place in Britain.

(i) Basle's unique Assembly

The Basle European Ecumenical Assembly held in May 1989 brought together 700 delegates from Roman Catholic, Orthodox, Anglican and Protestant churches in Europe. It was co-sponsored by the Conference of European Churches and the European Catholic Bishops Conference, with equal representations from each. Paul Hypher, a member of the Bishops' Conference of England and Wales, commented on the participation of Roman Catholics as follows:

> Basle proved that Roman Catholics need not be afraid of such gatherings and also that it is completely possible for the Roman Catholic Church to forge a broad alliance with other Christians on justice and peace issues. I believe if Roman Catholics had been absent the Assembly would have been weakened. There is a clear complementarity between the Roman Catholic emphasis on creational and sacramental theology and the Reformed

emphasis on penance and conversion. Basle also demonstrated a particular affinity between the Roman Catholic and Othodox churches.

Church leaders from different traditions chaired the main sessions under the overall moderatorship of Cardinal Martini of Milan and Metropolitan Alexi of Leningrad (now Patriarch of the Russian Orthodox Church). The session which produced the final document *Peace with Justice for the Whole Creation* was chaired by John Arnold, Dean of Durham. Ninety-five per cent of the delegates voted for it, and the two-page summary was approved by ninety-eight per cent – an impressive consensus.

Speeches and resolutions were interspersed with symbolic acts, such as the peace walk across the frontiers of three countries. Delegates commented on the effectiveness of these in underlining what was being communicated verbally in the main conference.

The Assembly made several affirmations and a group of recommendations for action with regard to justice, peace and the environment. The general affirmations included the following: sharing resources with the poor and oppressed and working for a new international economic order, supporting human rights, developing a new partnership between humanity and nature, working for the non-violent resolution of conflicts, and committing ourselves to a new life-style in our churches, societies, families and communities.

As Christians we are living in God's covenant with us and the whole of creation. We are all part of the one body of Christ. Because God changes hearts and minds, we covenant with one another. Our first loyalty belongs to him. All other loyalties (national, cultural, social, etc.) are of secondary importance. This is the basis for our engagement for justice, peace and the integrity of creation.

Recommendations for justice included commitment to sustainable development, regulation of international trade, ethical investment and restructured production and consumption. The poorest countries should be released from debt. Population policy should focus on economic and social development based on reverence for life. Work should be shared between men and women. The Single European Act of 1992 must not lead to a levelling down of social provisions or ecological standards and care must be exercised to protect refugees and migrant workers in and beyond Europe. European churches should support the people of Latin America, Africa and Asia in their struggle for justice, peace and the preservation of their environment.

Recommendations for peace focussed on the continuation of disarmament negotiations, a comprehensive Test Ban on nuclear weapons, abstention from the military use of space or Antarctica and the outlawing of weapons of mass destruction. The export of weapons and weapons technology to conflict zones should stop, defensive systems of security should be developed, and arms industries should be converted into civil production. The rights of conscientious objectors should be recognised, churches should forge peace partnerships across European borders, and peace education with emphasis on conflict resolution should be promoted in church and society. Christians must renounce violence in their own lives.

Recommendations concerning the environment included the reduction of energy use and the promotion of energy saving policies, the development of renewable energy supplies and the phasing out of nuclear power. Measures must be taken to protect the ozone layer, reduce the greenhouse effect, and preserve the rain forests. International agreements are needed on waste disposal, border-crossing emissions, genetic engineering and species preservation.

A major strength of the final Assembly document was that following brief explanatory paragraphs about justice, peace and threats to the environment ('integrity of creation' was not used), the interrelationships between the three elements were stressed, with specific examples:

> The interlocking dimensions of the crisis can only be shown by some examples. As a first illustration we choose the connection between economic injustice and deforestation in the Amazon region. The debt crisis severely affects Brazil. A large part of the debt was incurred by military spending and was partly used to develop the Brazilian arms industry. Efforts to repay the debts particularly harm the poor. The failure to implement land reform has meant that settlers move into the rain forest. The way of life of the indigenous population is severely disrupted and threatened. Transnational corporations too have bought up large areas of forest which they clear. This has led to a dramatic loss of genetic resources. Burning of wood has a damaging effect on the world's atmosphere.[65]

The greenhouse effect was carefully considered by a group of Canadian and European delegates who covenanted together to urge their churches to adopt policy statements and share information about this problem, and to explore the possibility of a future meeting at which the greenhouse gas issue might be subsumed under the broader topic of energy policy – which some churches, at least, have mechanisms for discussing.

65 *Peace with Justice*, Conference of European Churches, 1989, p. 37.

The document attributes the reasons for the current global crises to human attitudes and mentalities which require radical conversion:

The real causes, however, are to be sought in the very heart of humankind, in human attitudes and mentalities. There is the illusion that human beings are capable of shaping the world . . . that the created world has been put into our hands for exploitation rather than for care and cultivation; the blind confidence that new discoveries will solve problems as they arise and the subsequent neglect of the risks which have been brought about by our own actions. There is a clear need for the resources of science and technology as we face the future. But if we are to serve the cause of justice, peace and the preservation of the environment, the expectations they have generated must be radically re-evaluated. As Christians, we cannot uncritically advocate an ideology of human progress which of itself does not take adequate account of the whole person . . . We believe that it is through conversion to Christ that we shall discover the full meaning of human life.[66]

This emphasis upon conversion was an important aspect of the Assembly, echoing James Baldwin's speech about racism at the 1968 WCC Uppsala Assembly: 'I tremble when I wonder if there is left in the Christian civilisation, the moral energy, the spiritual daring, to atone, to repent, to be born again.'

(ii) **A vision of Europe**

The Report's section, 'Towards a Vision of Europe', was written prior to the collapse of the Berlin Wall. It calls for a healing of divisions, disarmament, the protection of minorities and refugees, and the establishment of a European Open House characterised by the following 'house rules':

− The principle of equality of all who live in Europe, whether strong or weak;

− The recognition of such values as freedom, justice, tolerance, solidarity, and participation;

− A positive attitude towards adherents of different religions, cultures and world views;

− Open doors, open windows − in other words: many personal contacts; exchange of ideas. Conflicts must be resolved through dialogue and not violence.

66 *Ibid.*, p. 38.

With reference to the Single European Act, the Report has this to say:
The Single European Act, which aims at a barrier free market in
the European Community after 1992, is already dynamising the
process of Western European integration. This raises both
expectations and anxieties. The hope is that the well-being of
many people will be improved. The fear is that this will happen
at the expense of and at the exclusion of many others. As
churches in Europe as a whole we must advocate that this
opening up of the borders within Western Europe does not lead
to a 'bastion Western Europe' which becomes more closed
towards the rest of the world. Economic cooperation, including
measures to ameliorate the debt crisis, and also to lessen the
technological gap between Western Europe and Eastern Europe
and between Northern and Southern Europe are required. The
same applies to other issues. The policy towards refugees and
asylum seekers especially will be a test of this openness.
Moreover, the churches in the countries directly involved must
be especially attentive to the effects of this integration on the
North-South relations within Europe, on the needs of the poor
within their own societies, on social security and on participation,
and on the needs of nature to be respected and protected.[67]

This is a key section of the Report, and deserves careful scrutiny. The
Euro-Community currently accounts for 37% of all world trade and buys
more than 20% of Third World exports. Will 'the rising tide lift all boats',
so that all will benefit from the prosperity expected to follow the removal
of European trade barriers? Or will disparities soon appear comparable to
the ones which followed the implementation of 'trickle-down' theories of
economic growth? Non-governmental organisations such as Christian Aid
are already pressing for cost-benefit surveys of the likely effects of
unification on issues such as the import of processed food from developing
countries.

In chapter two, section (iv), reference was made to ill health in
Southeast Asia resulting from the use of excessive quantities of
monosodium glutamate (MSG) in food. The background to this problem
illustrates our present concern. For many years Thai farmers converted
land for food into large areas for growing tapioca, which was then exported
to Europe as cattle feed. But after some time during which the Thais used
their European currency obtained by selling tapioca to pay for technological know-how, the French suddenly decided that they would supply all
cattle feed within the European Community. Unfortunately land used to

67 Ibid., p. 51.

grow tapioca is very difficult to convert back to use for something else, and the Thais were therefore left with an enormous surplus.

But then the Japanese company Ajinomoto offered to buy up all the tapioca and convert it in Southeast Asian factories into MSG for use as a food additive. They also wanted an advertising campaign to encourage people to sprinkle MSG more liberally on their food. But nobody told the Thais that excessive use of MSG can cause brain damage and cancer, and that children are especially at risk.

In the light of such unfortunate repercussions of a decision made in Europe one might hope that members of the new European governing bodies will all sit beneath metal plaques saying: 'Think JPIC'!

Another important issue which could be influenced by changes in European policy is the repayment of debts by developing countries to the international banks. The Basle recommendations call for an urgent solution to this problem:

> For the debt crisis, we recommend that the poorest developing countries be released from their debts, while effective measures are taken towards the alleviation of the debt of all indebted countries, including those in Eastern Europe. Governments are in a position to cancel or reschedule debts and to assist commercial banks and international institutions undertaking similar actions. Conditions should be created to prevent these countries from getting indebted again to the current extent . . . and to make sure that the funds released are being used for the benefit of the victims of poverty.[68]

But what will happen to policies concerning these debts if European banks amalgamate to produce a smaller number of more powerful and autonomous institutions? And why should funds released via the amelioration of the debt crisis be used solely for the victims of poverty? Might not a proportion also go towards the resolution of environmental problems?

Will the increased participation of Eastern Europe and the collapse of the former USSR result in the diversion of aid, personnel, investment and attention from the Third World? It is hard to imagine that Britain could invest less in the Third World than at present, but it will be increasingly hard to improve current levels of British support if Eastern Europe also makes substantial claims. In this respect it is instructive to compare Eastern Europe and the Third World from the point of view of deaths per thousand of children under the age of five. In Britain the number is 11; in Eastern Europe the corresponding figures are: Poland 18, Romania 28.

68 *Ibid.*, p. 56.

In many developing countries the corresponding figures are much higher: Brazil 77, India 149, Ethiopia 259, and Mozambique 298 (aggravated by war). Such figures provide a much more reliable indicator of where aid priority should lie than fluctuating political realignments, sudden disasters, etc.

The Basle document considered many of the structural economic causes of Third World poverty. But it did not address some of the fundamental causes of injustice arising from the uses of certain forms of technology.

Consider, for example, the imbalance between Europe and Southeast Asia in relation to the microelectronics industry. We have seen how Malaysian sweatshops are complemented by the more acceptable face of the same industries in Scotland. When participants from the Glasgow consultation visited a local electronics factory they were told by an enthusiastic personnel officer that the workforce were so ecstatically happy that it had never even entered their heads to form a union. We may or may not believe this, but there is no doubt that the absence of effective unions in factories run by the same firms in Southeast Asia is for totally different reasons.

But apart from these problems, some of which may be mitigated as a result of common action by European unions, there is an additional element of exploitation in some technologies. This was made very clear by Stephen Maxwell, an organiser for Scottish Education and Action for Development, during the Glasgow consultation:

> The challenge which the electronics revolution presents to the developing nations is not limited to manufacturing. Perhaps the most crucial impact of electronics will be in the new information industries.
>
> The convergence of electronic information processing, data banks and telecommunication systems into a single information network is a development of fundamental importance to third world development prospects. The global information network which has been created is a monopoly of developed countries, substantially of United States multinational companies. While the Third World has 78% of the world's population, generates 20% of world trade and is responsible for 12–13% of the world's industrial output, it has only 7% of the world's telephones, 6% of computers, 3% of research and development expenditure and 5% of science and technology publications.
>
> In this network the developing country has two roles – as a supplier of raw data on everything from mineral resources and crop forecasts to market surveys, government expenditure programmes and credit ratings, and as a recipient of processed

information and other media products. But while it supplies much of the information unpaid, even as with satellite surveillance of crop prospects, unwittingly, it has to pay for most of the processed information and media products it takes from the global network . . .

The implications of the developed country control of the global information network spread beyond economics to the cultural and political. The cultural issue has surfaced in calls sponsored by UNESCO for a New World Information Order strengthening national communications networks, particularly in the flow of information, and ideas and cultural values from North to South.

For a third world electronics producer like Malaysia, it is a cruel irony – it supplies the cheap labour to make the electronic components which when put to work in manufacturing and the new information industries confirm its dependence and increase its vulnerability to exploitation.[69]

Such latent injustices within certain technologies must be teased out and discussed in addition to the more blatant and visible ones. The transfer of technology between North and South is a major item on the agenda of the Rio de Janeiro Earth Summit.

Michael Smart has written perceptively about the importance of broadening the British debate about peace to make room for arguments that life would be better for everyone in the absence of armaments:

Armaments do not in themselves cause wars, nor, except on an unacceptably simplistic argument, are they the sole or even main cause of other evils to which humanity is subject, whether hunger and poverty or racial, sexual and social injustice. Connections need to be made and it is not easy for politicians arguing in an adversarial situation to find the time or inclination to tease them out.[70]

It is precisely at this point that the churches, with their vision of the totality and interrelatedness of creation, have an important role in studying and pointing out these connections.

From a somewhat different angle Irish ecumenist David Bleakley praised the Basle peace discussions for introducing a 'paradigm shift' away from the just war theory: 'For me as a pacifist a breakthrough came when

69 Stephen Maxwell, 'International Perspectives: Malaysia's Electronics Industry', in Howard Davis and David Gosling, eds., Will the Future Work?, WCC, Geneva, 1986, p. 69.
70 Michael Smart, 'Peace and the Churches: Notes for an Agenda', in the Modern Churchman, Vol. 30, No. 3, 1988, p. 1.

the centrality of the just war theory was dropped in favour of a just peace imperative,' he said.

In addition to such global justice and peace issues there are many others of a more domestic nature. For example, it is important to ask whether or not the three hundred or so European laws to be agreed before the end of 1992 represent a harmonisation of existing policies for the admission and exclusion of immigrants and refugees, or will there be a settlement in favour of the most easily negotiable lowest common policy, which is bound to be the toughest one?

(iii) Our Common Future

In her foreword to the British Government's response to *Our Common Future*, the Report of the World Commission on Environment and Development, Margaret Thatcher endorses the concept of sustainable development which she describes as 'the central message of the Report'.[71] Sustainable development is 'development that meets the needs of the present without compromising the ability of future generations to meet their own needs', a process of change 'in which the exploitation of resources, the direction of investments, the orientation of technological development and institutional change are made consistent with future as well as with present needs'.

Fine words. But as Sir Walter Scott was fond of observing, 'fine words butter no parsnips'. More concretely, sustainable development means several things. We must care for the basic assets of humanity, which are the air, water, soil fertility and the productivity of our crops, trees and livestock. We must use the products of nature in a durable manner and set development goals that fit within nature's limits, which are known to scientists and have been understood by many people all over the world for generations. We must devise humane, effective policies to limit population growth so as to bring human numbers into stable balance with the earth that sustains them, and we must ensure that the biosphere continues to function in an overall stable and predictable manner.

Critics of the *Brundtland Report*, as it is often named after its chairperson, Mrs Gro Harlem Brundtland, are uneasy about its central arguments about the relationship between sustainability and economic growth. According to Jonathon Porritt:

> The lack of intellectual rigour on . . . the compatibility between economic growth and ecological sustainability is most disturbing.

71 Margaret Thatcher, letter dated July 1988, in *Our Common Future, a Perspective by the United Kingdom on the Report of the World Commission on Environment and Development*, Department of the Environment, 1988.

To bewail the devastating impact of conventional, growth-driven development policies on the environment of many Third World countries; to leap promptly from these to an embarrassingly ardent advocacy of accelerated rates of growth in the world economy; and then to attempt to bridge this divide by piously hoping that the growth process will be appropriately tempered . . . can only be described as a deliberate, politically-expedient cop-out.[72]

The Basle document calls for sustainability with regard to social and international relationships, the environment, economics and between generations, but somehow misses out on the *Brundtland Report*'s overall ethical principle that present actions must not foreclose future options. Thus the Basle Report is not clear how 'priority for the poor, the oppressed and the powerless' relates to economic development which has to be submitted to criteria for the various types of sustainability listed above.[73]

The seeming reluctance of the Basle document either to endorse fully the *Brundtland Report* or to provide a satisfactory alternative definition of sustainability means that the environmental recommendations lack a coherent framework and rationale. No justification is given for the view that 'nuclear power should not be the basis of future energy supply because of its social, technical, ecological and military risks'. What about the enormous risks and environmental damage caused by coal burning? And although Europeans may themselves be willing to accept whatever reduction in standards of living may result from the abandonment of nuclear power, ought one to expect the same sacrifices from populations for whom any reduction in standards of living means certain death for many more than might be at risk on account of the operation of nuclear power plants (e.g. in Indonesia)?

The *Brundtland Report*'s call for a drastic reduction in energy consumption in industrialised countries is enthusiastically commended in the Basle document:

The wasteful use of energy in the industrialised countries has reached such gigantic proportions that there is an urgent need for a drastic reduction in their use. Some churches have committed themselves to work for a significant reduction in the use of energy. We appeal to all the European churches and

72 Jonathon Porritt, Review of *Our Common Future*, quoted in *Green Christians*, Newsletter of Christian Ecology Link, February/April, 1990, p. 9.
73 *Op. cit.* (61), p. 55.

Christians to do the same within the limit of their possibilities and untiringly to challenge decision-makers in political, technological and business life to more efficient policies for saving energy . . . According to the *Brundtland Report* the technical possibility exists of reducing per capita energy consumption in industrialised countries by 50% and increasing the per capita energy consumption in the Third World countries by 30% (on the basis of predictable increases in population). In so doing the total world energy consumption would only be increased insignificantly. This is the only worldwide energy perspective which should be considered seriously by Christians in the industrialised countries, particularly as the *Brundtland Report* has increased substantially public awareness of ecological issues and is well regarded in the scientific community.[74]

The subsequent recommendation says that 'special measures have urgently to be taken in order to protect the ozone layer, to counteract the greenhouse effect, preserve what is left of the rain forest, and to prevent the spread of desertification'. All very commendable, but would it not also be helpful to know roughly to what extent the proposed reductions in energy consumption will reduce carbon dioxide emissions and hence provide even greater incentives to implement them? Recent estimates by a Cambridge scientist suggest that a fairly well-off British family produces about seven times the average global per capita release of carbon dioxide, mostly through travel, heating and cooking.[75] Thus if we can conserve energy by, say insulating our homes, we may release scarce fuel resources to enable developing countries to provide cheap electricity for their cities, at the same time reducing carbon dioxide build-up which, if allowed to continue unchecked, will cause global warming, expansion of water and melting of glaciers and the polar icecaps, and the submersion of many low-lying land formations, ultimately including perhaps even Cambridge and the Fens!

No doubt the Basle Assembly participants would protest that their recommendations were never intended for such close scrutiny and were more in the nature of guidelines to churches. But it cannot be emphasised too strongly that it is the interconnections between the various problems under consideration that require elucidation, and that to 'think JPIC' means to tease out the details and to act on the basis of the total picture thereby obtained.

74 *Ibid.*, p. 61.
75 Ian and Pearl Woodward, 'Warming to the greenhouse effect' in *Spotlight*, Great St Mary's, the University Church, Cambridge, 1990, p. 15.

(iv) Secular ethics

It will be interesting to see whether or not the progressive unification of Europe produces any kind of consensus with regard to ethics. Whatever their official religious affiliation most European states are now essentially secular. It was interesting, therefore, at Basle to hear a strong plea for a system of theocentric ethics similar in many respects to that of the last chapter by Archbishop Kirill of Smolensk. His argument merits careful consideration, and is therefore quoted in full:

> In order to avoid relativism, Christian ethics should not lose its basic orientation with regard to values. And theocentrism provides such an orientation. The theocentric ethic, stressing wholeness, interconnectedness and the value of the whole creation, considers nature and man not as autonomous and self-contained entities, but as the elements finding their meaning and purpose in the Creator. Such ethics, while overcoming anthropocentrism, do not run to the opposite extreme and avoid the emphasis on the autonomous importance of nature, as it would mean 'naturocentrism', a new paganism.
>
> The theocentric ethics must establish the real balance between humankind and nature, stressing the fact that all creation has one purpose – the glorification of the Creator. Both humankind and nature, approaching the Creator, find their meaning in their transfiguration. Such ethics attach value to both and subordinate them to the supreme value – God. At the same time, the human being is treated as a quite special element, elevated above all creation, remaining, however, part of the one, interconnected, and organically whole world in which nature has its own value. Nature ceases to be just an object used by humankind for its purpose. These ethics make it possible to help people overcome the contemporary crises, as they presuppose the rejection of the human drive to dominate nature.
>
> And this calls for a voluntary limitation of consumption, simplicity in one's lifestyle, a careful use of science and technology, respect for life, economy in the use of resources and their fair distribution for the benefit of all.
>
> This last element must be underlined. Theocentric ethics are not limited by ecology. They cultivate respect for life and freedom of all beings. The moral aspects of the 'integrity of creation' are closely connected with the notions of 'peace' and 'justice'.

Archbishop Kirill goes on to consider what this means for inter-faith and Christian/Marxist dialogue:

At the same time one must remember that theocentric ethics are religious ethics and as such may be unacceptable for non-religious people. And here the problem arises: How can Christians, without digressing from the principles of these ethics, cooperate with people of other religions and ideologies? Obviously, there must be some general elements as a basis for such cooperation.

Common concern is the main element of this common character. Christians must find ways to communicate and cooperate with all those who share their concern with regard to the state of human civilisation. This calls for wisdom and a careful choice in the language and the use of arguments.

On this path arises the indispensable question of a broader, not only pan-Christian, but of a truly global consensus. Without a rationally expressed consensus it is difficult to wager upon the success of joint actions of people of different religious, ideological and political views, belonging to various nations and cultures. It seems that the only possible consensus is the moral one, based on absolute moral values . . . The introduction of the notion of the absolute into the ethics bridges the gap separating Christians and Marxists, believers and non-believers, thus forming the focus of this common ethical consensus. Each of the sides may use its own language, but it is important that these languages should describe one and the same system of moral values having the absolute at its centre.

This consensus will be really theocentric for a Christian, while a Marxist will characterise it as a moral system, subordinate to the idea of the absolute human universal values. It is important to keep this system free from relativism. Thus the common understanding of morality and the corresponding assessment of human experience will make universal dialogue possible . . .

The human conscience has a tremendous importance in all this. The common character of conscience unites all people and helps them in their quest for truth, as well as in finding solutions to moral problems. It is well known that the conscience may be affected by sin, but despite this, it remains the only human ability through which the moral law implanted by God into human nature can be discovered. The conscience is capable of limiting desires, challenging egos to shape human behaviour. That is why special attention must be paid today to the ecology of human conscience. Keeping and safeguarding the conscience of the modern human being is, finally, the concern for justice, peace and the integrity of creation, as without conscience it is impossible to implement even the noblest moral consensus.[76]

It is interesting to compare Archbishop Kirill's arguments with those of Göran Collste in chapter three, as well as with the section on theocentric ethics in the last chapter. His appeal to moral values and use of concepts such as transfiguration enables him to remain firmly within the Russian Orthodox tradition while finding common ground with many other points of view, both religious and secular.

One of the Basle working groups made Archbishop Kirill's address the basis for a four stage approach to ecumenical ethics, as follows:

(1) First comes the common concern in recognising the dangers to which we are exposed;

(2) Next we must arrive at a moral consensus based on absolute moral values and belonging to the whole human family;

(3) In searching for the truth and in solving moral problems we are assisted by the human conscience;

(4) The conscience needs to be educated and trained.

With regard to the relationship between Christian and secular ethics the working group made three points:

– As Christians we know we are on a common road with all people of goodwill. Faith in Jesus Christ shows *us* the goal, provides the motivation and reveals to us the meaning of the road we are travelling along.

– As Christians we stand *within the world*. Faith in Jesus Christ indicates the values which guide us in our efforts to order the world. It can also reinforce promptings coming from outside. The call for solidarity, for example, can be adopted and enriched by the Christian obligation to practice love of the neighbour.

– As Christians we are united with hosts of other human beings in the same society in process of change. Faith in Jesus Christ can become a critical reference point which unmasks this society's ideologies and introduces to it a special sensibility to peace, justice and life.

The group recognised the danger of 'cheating' our consciences (Bonhoeffer), the need for mutual correction, and the existence of 'structures of sin'. In the face of these 'we are summoned to repentance and conversion'.[77]

Recommendations such as these could provide the kind of foundational basis for action which was advocated in the last chapter.

The Basle document has been formally welcomed by the British Council of Churches (now the Council of Churches for Britain and Ireland, with

76 Archbishop Kirill, *Op. cit.* (61), p. 170.
77 *Op. cit.* (61), p. 125.

full Roman Catholic participation) and commended to the churches for study in the hope that JPIC 'will be a major focus of the agendas of the new ecumenical instruments'.

(v) British JPIC initiatives

Writing in the *Independent* about the choice of an Archbishop of Canterbury, Monica Furlong had this to say –

My dearest hope . . . is that we might get an Archbishop who will see women's issues as connected, indeed intrinsic to problems of poverty, developing countries, the family, the development of children . . . Occasionally a bishop . . . talks about women's issues as if they might be a key to much that ails us all spiritually, ecologically, developmentally, as if he believes that what is said and done by the Church in this area might actually *matter*.[78]

In other words, the ideal Archbishop should be a JPIC type of person.

British people have great difficulty in assimilating the kind of slogans that international organisations such as the WCC tend to propagate. But we have tried to demonstrate that JPIC is about vital issues in today's world which are inseparable from one another and must be addressed together. In this section a brief review will be made of British church activities which have been conceived in terms of JPIC. There are, as yet, very few.

From what was said earlier about Scottish involvement in ecumenical work it is not surprising that the Scottish Churches Group on JPIC has been functioning for several years. It aims 'to give stimulus and added strength to the churches' existing efforts in the field, by putting them in closer touch with one another and by setting them in the context of the international process, so that they can give to it and receive from it'.

Alison Elliot, the Group's secretary, described the Group's primary role as educational. An attractive pack *While Earth Endures . . .* has been prepared to demonstrate how justice, peace and environmental issues are associated, and to encourage local initiatives.[79] A session on Creation suggested in the pack begins by affirming that 'human beings share in God's creative activity – that is what it means to be created in His image. We do it through the arts . . ., science . . ., through ordinary activities like the keeping of gardens, photography . . .' Bible study passages explore the themes of dominion, exploitation, partnership and community, and there are useful quotes by Robert Burns ('thy poor earth-born companion

78 Monica Furlong in the *Independent*, 13.4.90, p. 21.
79 *While Earth Endures . . .*, Centre for JPIC, Scottish Churches Council, Dunblane, 1989.

and fellow mortal') and from the *Brundtland Report*. Finally, the reader is invited to do one or two things individually and as part of a group 'that can contribute to the safeguarding of Creation for the future'.

First Things First, a selection of study guides for congregations produced by the former British Council of Churches and Christian Aid, is similar in scope and includes an interesting case study based on a predominantly black Caribbean community church in North London.[80]

Tony Addy, director of the William Temple Foundation in Manchester, has become involved in JPIC from the point of entry of unemployment, a concern which began at meetings in Driebergen (Netherlands) and Manchester in 1985 and 1986 leading to the establishment of a West European Network on Work, Unemployment and the Churches. A more recent meeting took place in 1988 at the Evangelische Akademie at Mulheim, and there were a number of informal caucuses at the Basle Assembly. Members of the network are concerned that, just as United Europe should not aggravate poverty in the Third World, so it must also not increase the gap between rich and poor within its own boundaries.

Michael Plunkett, Churches Healthy Cities Link Officer in Merseyside, has devised an imaginative programme linking health problems in major British cities to both JPIC and the World Health Organisation's Health 2000 programme. The three cities so far adopted are Liverpool, Glasgow and Belfast, but more than seventy city health authorities have expressed interest. The Healthy Cities pack for parishes contains practical suggestions for improving health, and challenges popular fallacies such as the view: 'It's my body and what I do with it is nobody's business but mine'. A healthy city is described as a place which shapes human possibility, and experience has a crucial role to play in determining the health of city dwellers. The need for justice – evidenced by the fact that ill health and poverty go hand in hand, peace – the recognition that all things have fulfilment both within themselves and externally, and a supportive environment, are essential prerequisites for sound health.

The United Reformed Church (URC) produced a popular JPIC leaflet in the autumn of 1988 and has also distributed a summary of *Our Common Future* which places its recommendations within the context of JPIC. Negotiations are in progress for the URC to become a Just Peace Church similar to its counterpart in the USA, but the final decision is conditional on congregational approval.

The Quakers have produced a JPIC workshop and information pack and have recently conducted a survey of JPIC-related activities among their

80   *First Things First,* BCC and Christian Aid, 1989.

local groups. The most frequently mentioned organised activities were Traidcraft, support for Amnesty International and letter writing on subjects as diverse as the arms trade, radioactive waste dumping and the detention of children in South Africa. Reference was also made to the use of the Meeting House as a community resource and the encouragement of planet-friendly practices such as recycling paper, not using ozone-damaging CFC's and using biodegradable household goods.

The Methodists have 'borrowed' and modified the Quaker JPIC pack for their own use. But by and large they have so far regarded JPIC as essentially what they are doing already. Their Working Party on the Environment and the Church of England's Environmental Issues Reference Panel have ensured that both churches are encouraged to take the environmental component of JPIC at least as seriously as the other two.

The Church of England's official response to JPIC has so far been shaped by the Lambeth Conference. Recognising that 'a proper under-standing of the doctrine of creation carries with it important ethical considerations about the behaviour of humanity in relation to technology and the environment', the Conference identified four inter-related areas which threaten life: the unjust distribution of the world's wealth, social injustice within nations, the rise of militarism and irreversible damage to the environment. It called for study, reflection and action on these issues, the commendation of *Our Common Future* and participation in the JPIC process.[81]

Two important statements were issued by the Roman Catholic Church and the Ecumenical Patriarchate respectively towards the end of 1989, which, although not couched in JPIC language, echo similar ideas. In a message dated December 8th, 1989, for the New Year celebration of the World Day of Peace, the Pope drew attention to the growth of recent ecological awareness as a means of achieving peace. Building on the words of the Second Vatican Council, 'God destined the earth and all it contains for the use of every individual and all peoples', he challenged the unjust accumulation of resources and goods by a privileged few, and called for international, national and personal action to avert a crisis.

The Ecumenical Patriarch, in a message dated September 1st, 1989, had less to say about the justice and peace dimensions of the ecological crisis, but made some striking observations about the way Orthodox liturgy expresses many of our current concerns and our potential priestly role in redeeming the whole of creation:

81 *The Truth Shall Make You Free*, Report of the 1988 Lambeth Conference, Church House Publishing, London, 1988, p. 174, 229.

Just as the priest at the Eucharist offers the fullness of creation and receives it back as the blessing of Grace in the form of the consecrated bread and wine, to share with others, so we must be the channel through which God's grace and deliverance is shared with all creation. The human being is simply yet gloriously the means for the expression of creation in its fullness and the coming of God's deliverance for all creation.[82]

The Irish churches have so far said little about the JPIC process as such, though the Politics and Forgiveness Project and several studies of peacemaking emphasise the justice element of all peace initiatives. Reporting on the Basle Assembly, John May from the Irish School of Ecumenics noted that British and Irish delegates experienced great difficulty discussing the situation in Northern Ireland. He writes: 'If Europeans cannot discuss openly their own endemic trouble spots, what they have to say about social, political and environmental problems elsewhere will not have much credibility'.

During the period leading up to the Earth Summit a good deal is being said about the environmental implications of Third World debts and their impact on local economies. Christian Aid points out that in Bolivia, for example, more people work in the 'informal' than in the 'formal' sector of the economy, earning their living from foreign currency as hawkers, car attendants, prostitutes and cocaine traffickers. [83] It has been claimed that cocaine alone brings more foreign exchange into Bolivia than all her legal exports put together.

Whether the activities which have been described are related explicitly to JPIC or not, the extent to which they may be regarded as covenants is not very clear. The Basle Assembly said a good deal about commitments, but a commitment is not the same as a covenant, which is binding on all parties and involves their active consent.

We shall return to this point in the last chapter; in the next section consideration will be given to some recent religious affirmations on the environment, some of which relate more explicitly to peace and justice issues than others.

(vi) **Enlarging the framework**

In September 1986 the World Wide Fund for Nature (then the World Wildlife Fund) marked its twenty-fifth anniversary with an interfaith celebration of creation at Assisi. The five religions officially represented were Christianity (the Minister General of the Franciscans attended),

82 Ecumenical Patriarchate, *Harvest Message*, September 1st, 1989.
83 *Banking on the Poor*, Christian Aid, 1988, p. 16.

Tibetan Buddhism, Hinduism, Islam and Judaism. There were five separate liturgies, each of which contained an expression of the relationship between religious faith and the Earth, and the importance of living together harmoniously. The event marked a new phase in interfaith dialogue and created possibilities for enlarging the framework of JPIC thinking and types of activities.

In September 1989 the British Council of Churches and the World Wide Fund for Nature jointly sponsored a conference on Christian Faith and Ecology to coincide with a Festival of Faith and the Environment in Canterbury. Seven major world religions were represented. The gathering as a whole was marked by a spirit of humility and cooperation and a sense that differences can be overcome by sharing and through practical concern for the world's problems. In his address the Archbishop of Canterbury told the congregation:

> The conviction that nature does not exist simply and solely for the benefit of humankind . . . is becoming increasingly widespread and articulate. Because it finds its true source at such deep levels of the human spirit, it must, I think, be called a religious conviction. But it is not a conviction unique to any one religion in particular, and it is shared by some who would profess no religion at all.

Sunday worship took the form of a Creation Eucharist, which included some interesting material such as the recasting of the traditional *Benedicite* as a lament for our despoiled world:

> And I, the earth the Lord created,
> Cry to him who made me,
> Save me from ravage and destruction
> To praise and glorify thy name forever.[84]

The Assisi and Canterbury events were major occasions on which leaders of different religious traditions expressed their concern for the environment and pledged themselves to protect it. In October 1987 there was an imaginative Creation Harvest Liturgy in Winchester Cathedral at which representatives of Buddhism, Bahai, Hinduism, Islam, Judaism, Sikhism and Taoism were present.

The Catholic Fund for Overseas Development (CAFOD) has produced some excellent liturgical and study material which emphasises the need to see environmental and development problems as justice issues.[85] Their

84 *Creation Eucharist,* Festival of Faith and the Environment, 1989, p. 5.
85 *Celebrating One World: A Resource Book on Liturgy and Social Justice,* CAFOD and Thomas More Centre, 1987, and *Renewing the Earth, Study Guide for Groups,* CAFOD, 1987.

publications contain a comprehensive list of other materials available. The United Reformed Church has very recently produced a beautifully illustrated anthology of prose and poetry, prayers and hymns on the theme of creation and the environment, and the Methodists have followed up their widely-circulated tape-slide 'Making Peace with the Planet' with worship material designed to explore the urban and sea-faring environments of Liverpool and the Shetlands.[86] Tear Fund has produced materials for children and some imaginative display materials suitable for harvest exhibitions.[87]

These are some recent attempts by British churches and organisations to express the view that creation is one and that religions must pool their resources in order to find common solutions to the world's problems. Collectively they represent a move away from anthropocentrism to an affirmation of the intrinsic value of all creation and therefore of all parts of humanity and all human groups. Thus creation becomes the springboard for justice and for peace, though not all three elements are emphasised in the above-mentioned activities and publications. But in spite of their tentativeness, they are unmistakable moves away from individualism to interdependence, a sense of the need to grow into God, and a consensus that we must act decisively now. Nature is increasingly recognised not as an unimportant appendage of humanity, but as an integral component of the seamless fabric of which we are a significant but not unduly dominant part. This view, which underlies much JPIC thinking, has been taken up by the late Mary Clare, former Mother Superior of the Sisters of the Love of God:

> We must try to understand the meaning of the age in which we are called to bear witness. We must accept the fact that this is an age in which the cloth is being unwoven. It is therefore no good trying to patch. We must, rather, set up the loom on which coming generations may weave new cloth according to the pattern God provides.[88]

As we enlarge our understanding we can expect to recognise relationships which sometimes oppress, sometimes offer new hopes for concerted action. That is what JPIC is all about.

86 *Threads of Creation: A Resource Book of Words and Pictures*, edited by John Reardon, United Reformed Church, 1989. *Harvest Pack 1988: Making Peace with the Planet*, Division of Social Responsibility, Methodist Church, March 1988.

87 *The Work of Our Hands*, Tear Fund, 1989.

88 Mother Mary Clare, *The Simplicity of Prayer*, SLG Press, Fairacres Publications, 1988.

6 Agenda for the Nineties

According to the Muslim academic and writer, Akbar Ahmed, 'The Third World cannot take seriously the green movement which in essence suggests their status quo'. A similar criticism could be levelled at church members who baptize the green movement insofar as it is concerned exclusively with the environment in order to persuade us that God/ Christianity/the Church is green. There can be no satisfactory solutions to the world's problems which do not take into account the structural links between the state of the environment and the systematic violations of justice and peace which occur in many parts of the world.

This has therefore not been yet another 'green' Christian book. We have considered the various ways in which environmental concern has developed in different parts of the world and the variety of responses. And we have tried to show that there is a community of interest between, say, Brazilians who care about their forests and people in low-lying areas of East Anglia or Bangladesh who are worried about sea level rises caused by global warming.

Put in theological terms, our growth in awareness of common problems and the recognition that we must resolve them together is a sign of peace, *shalom,* the wholeness and the future hope towards which God's creative spirit is drawing creation. The Church, whose duty it is to be a sign of the world's coming into being, tries to focus and interpret the yearnings of creation, inviting all people to be co-creators – or co-workers – in God's creative activity, which encompasses the whole world. But as we do so we collide with the dark forces of injustice and division . . .

The integrity of creation reminds us of our relationship with God, with each other and the world around us, and with God's creative spirit, transforming all things into the realisation of 'a vision which is discovered only through its own realisation'.

We will now consider the implications of previous chapters. We began by considering how, in Britain, concern for the state of the environment came into prominence in the late 1960s, and although temporarily obscured by the energy issue in the 1970s, was acknowledged by the time of the 1983 Vancouver Assembly as of comparable importance to justice (conceived primarily in terms of structural disparities between North and South), and peace (primarily in relation to the East/West armaments build-up).

Chapter two offered a theological framework for the three components of the Vancouver phrase along the lines just indicated and gave a definition of integrity of creation. It proceeded to summarise the various ways in which concern for the state of the environment has manifested itself in different parts of the world and responses by the churches and religious groups. It was suggested that it is at the *regional* level – Latin America, Europe, East/West Africa, Southeast Asia – that there is scope for the most fruitful exploration of new issues, and that there is no reason to expect global solutions, global theologies, etc. Unlike the pre-Vancouver Just, Participatory and Sustainable Society, JPIC does not presuppose such a view, and makes most sense at regional and local levels. JPSS was essentially 'top-down' and as such was resented especially by the Third World, whereas JPIC is a 'bottom-up' approach.

Chapter three considered specific environmental issues which were the subject of responses by the WCC from Geneva. The first of these, a case study from the Marshall Islands, further illustrated the diversity with which different parts of the world experience environmental problems, and how these inevitably move into areas of justice and peace. The response of the Marshallese – taking their health into their own hands – was an effective counter to the dependence foisted on them, and also demonstrated a powerful underlying 'theology of creation' with regard to health care.

Chapter four brought us to our central argument. Whereas in chapter two we saw that environmental concern stimulated churches to rediscover 'doctrines of' creation, our definition of integrity of creation calls for a more fundamental restructuring which places creation at the centre where it serves as a basis for justice and peace. The major part of the chapter tried to show what this means in terms of specific issues, such as the Protestant Work Ethic, which is based on a mechanistic view of people as individuals whose worth is defined according to economic criteria. The notion of men and women in community should become the basis of any new Christian work ethic. We developed this argument further in relation to computerisation, concluding that computers have tended to undermine the sense of work community and have increased the power of management.

Mechanistic views of life systems are responsible for much that is wrong with science and technology and the way they operate. According to Charles Birch such concepts must be replaced by an ecological model according to which relationships can be conceived both with reference to their total environment and also internally. Such an understanding of living organisms will enable us to appreciate them for what they truly are (our foundational view of creation). It is also more compatible with an integral relationship between God and creation (panentheism) than with the deistic idea that God made nature and then left it, save for periodic interventions.

In *The Other Side of 1984* Lesslie Newbigin claims that 'the greatest intellectual task facing the church is a new dialogue with science . . . for which the way has been prepared by profound changes in science (especially in physics) this century'.[89] On the basis of the most up-to-date research in sub-particular physics, John Polkinghorne argues for a universe 'something in between' mechanical and organic models. Such are the fundamental creative processes of the universe that we can consider ourselves potentially as co-creators with God in the realisation of an open future. To take responsibility for our lives (as in the Marshallese example) is to be in tune with nature's own most fundamental activities. Here again we are at variance with deism, with its interventions, dependence and, one might add, guilt.

Birch and Polkinghorne disagree over process philosophy but otherwise tend to assume a theological position broadly in line with that of many mainstream churches. But some theological traditions are less accommodating to their arguments, and in section (iv) of chapter four we considered how recent advances in biotechnology appear from the standpoint of Russian Orthodoxy. The Russians had little difficulty in accepting that there are 'grey areas' between non-life and life, which became part of an agreed interpretation of the integrity of creation. But they could not accept that human beings are co-creators with God, only co-workers. By contrast Roman Catholics appear to have difficulties with the 'grey areas' but accept co-creation – see, for example, Cardinal Sin's exposition of *Laborem Exercens* in section (i) of the same chapter.

In chapter four, section (v), we considered moral arguments for cancelling the debts of developing countries to the international banks. Our argument, essentially, was that if nature possesses intrinsic value, then its despoliation by industrial nations during the past forty or so years must be given a retrospective price tag which will cancel out the accumulated debts of developing countries during approximately the same period. This argument underlies CCBI's statement to the Rio de Janeiro UN Earth Summit.

In these various ways we considered the implications of our view that the integrity of creation is foundational. Other examples could be added.[90] But we hope enough has been said to distinguish between 'doctrines of' creation (in Cobb's sense) – which are rushed into service to prove that the Church knows how to be green – and a theology of creation whereby *everything* must be reconsidered from the perspective of the enduring relationships between God, humanity and nature.

89 Lesslie Newbigin, *The Other Side of 1984*, WCC, Geneva, 1984, p. 60.
90 David Gosling, 'Towards a Credible Ecumenical Theology of Nature', in the *Ecumenical Review*, Vol. 38, No. 3, July 1986, p. 329.

The final parts of chapter four reviewed the methodologies used to arrive at this understanding, and gave an account of James Gustafson's striking categorisation of four types of moral discourse: prophetic, narrative, ethical and policy (illustrated from the Marshalls case study). Reference was also made to Gustafson's use of David Tracy's 'analogical imagination', and it was suggested that methodologies which involve abstraction via generalised principles to projection onto new situations may be seriously flawed. This constituted another reason for suspecting global views of things and paved the way for an account of what so far has been the most successful JPIC event, the European Assembly in Basle.

The Basle Assembly (chapter five) highlighted major issues for the European churches as they encounter dramatic realignments and the prospect of the Single European Act. The connections between justice, peace and the environment were explored, appropriate covenants were agreed, and warnings were issued against the potential dangers of 'bastion Western Europe', with all that might mean for the suffering of the poor in developing countries and within Europe's own boundaries. Foundational notions were identified, such as our standing as Christians 'within the world, . . . on a common ground with all people of goodwill, . . . united with hosts of other human beings in the same society in process of change'.

The latter part of chapter five considered JPIC initiatives taking place in Britain and the recent spate of interest in the environment in church circles. Some feel the need to enlarge the framework of Christian thinking and activity in Britain, but there has so far been little effort to regard JPIC as anything more than an appendage to what most churches regard as more important priorities.

(i) Design for living

Writing in the *Independent*, John Crocker, minister of the Horsham United Reformed Church, expresses the optimism of many people that together we can make our world a better place:

> There is hope for the world. There is hope, which I believe God has given, for humankind. The grounds for the hope lie, at least in part, in the fact that we are becoming aware of the problems and that God has given us the science, the resources and the intelligence to care for the world.[91]

The official logo for Justice, Peace and the Integrity of Creation shows a broken chain surrounded by red and yellow buds; there is a dove and

91 John P. Crocker in *The Independent*, 2 January 1990, p. 18.

floating cross inside the chain, and longer, thorn-covered chains in the background (*see front cover*).

Consider first the broken chain. We have described some of the injustices which oppress large sections of humanity and are instrumental in causing widespread damage to our planet. Among them the legacy of debts by developing countries to the international banks is responsible for enormous human cost which spills over into almost every area encompassed by JPIC.

We have tried to show that a Christian understanding of the intrinsic value of all creation implies the redressing of past wrongs whereby industrial nations have exploited cheap labour and resources in the Third World and polluted vast tracts of land everywhere at no cost to themselves. This injustice must now be redressed via the negotiated cancellation of Third World debts according to internationally agreed criteria. There is also an urgent need to rethink the entire basis of economics from the point of view of its environmental implications.

Europeans would do well to remember that under the Marshall Aid Plan at the end of the Second World War, the USA contributed large sums of money to rebuild our shattered cities. None of this has been repaid, for which we owe an immense debt of gratitude to the USA. But from their point of view this gift has turned out to be an excellent investment because it has strengthened some of the USA's best trading partners and thus in the long run boosted their economy and helped to maintain levels of employment.

Just as the *Brandt Report*, for all its inadequacies, enabled a consensus to form among people whose views ranged from pragmatic self-interest to romantic idealism, might not a comparable major initiative now focus a similar convergence of opinion in favour of the negotiated cancellation of all Third World debts? This must be a major item on our agenda for the Nineties.

A reason why the Vancouver Assembly jettisoned the Just, Participatory and Sustainable Society may well be that all the links which many WCC constituencies were told to regard as binding the world together are actually experienced by them as oppressive and alienating. History and economics are two potent examples. But what about science, with its implicit mechanistic assumptions, and technology, which although in theory amenable to the realisation of a better world, in practice rumbles on under its own momentum and all too easily becomes the property of vested interests which assume the clothing of internationality to sidestep more localised accountability? We have also seen how divisive, and hence contrary to peace, an exported work ethic can be, and the damaging effects of types of science education which keep science and ethics in separate, watertight compartments so that implicit goals are never challenged and redefined.

Healthcare, which in the heyday of western missionary expansion was in part at least an expression of Christian compassion, is now sullied by the reckless export by drug companies of inappropriate medicines to developing countries. Even aid can be used to create and manipulate dependencies. Language and thought-forms can be oppressive: James Gustafson's questioning of the process of abstraction followed by projection deserves careful scrutiny.

History, economics, science, technology, healthcare, aid, language – the list could be extended – conspire to forge oppressive links which must be removed and replaced before those who suffer as a result of them can join hands with each other and with others across the globe. The Sustainable (global) Society in JPSS in the seventies was seen by many as little more than a mandate to extend the 'limits to growth' arguments of the early seventies to maintain existing unjust structures. A Nicaraguan consultant at the first Church and Society Working committee in Bossey listened politely to a meticulously documented exposition of the latest limits to growth argument by a Norwegian expert: 'What growth?' was his only comment. JPIC does not presuppose a global society, and is applicable at regional and local levels – as we have seen.

The red and yellow buds circumscribing the broken chain of the JPIC logo suggest the outward growth of people and nature into an infinite expanse of space:

> We seek in freedom space and scope for dreaming,
> and look for ground where trees and plants may grow . . .
> But there are walls that keep us all divided;
> we fence each other in with hate and war.
> Fear is the bricks and mortar of our prison,
> our pride of self the prison coat we wear.
> The love of God is broad like beach and meadow,
> wide as the wind, and an eternal home.[92]

No external deity beckons, but a small, vulnerable, floating cross at the logo's centre reminds us of our pilgrimage together in the company of the dove which is God's way of existing in the world as the Holy Spirit. This enables us to be co-creators (or co-workers if our Orthodox friends prefer it) with God in activities the openness of which is evidenced by even the most recent research in physics.

The space surrounding the logo and the outward growth of the buds reminds us of the inclusiveness of our faith and the Church's mandate to

---

92 Lars Lundberg, 'The love of God', in *Cantate Domino*, Bärenreiter-Verlag Kassel, FRG, 1974, p. 86.

affirm every part of creation, beginning with the least and most despised. The distant thorn-covered chains represent our unfinished agenda.

An appealing picture, but what precisely are we to *do?*

Understand, and covenant. We defined a covenant as a binding agreement between two or more parties, but there have so far been few concrete examples.

'You shall be my people, and I will be your God', is the great covenant. Should we now effectively say to our world: 'You shall be our source of sustenance and of a secure future, and we will be your steward/priest/companion'?

We saw in chapter five some examples of JPIC initiatives in Britain especially in relation to unemployment, healthcare and environmental issues in Scotland, and it is hoped that there will be many more such activities as British churches become part of a wider JPIC process.

But unless there is to be an arbitrary proliferation of local initiatives, some guidelines and coordination will be necessary. It is hoped that the chapters of this book will provide useful information in this respect.

To give some concrete examples. The letter quoted at the beginning of this section continued as follows:

> A particular concern of mine is for the 110 million people of Bangladesh among whom I used to work. Their country is already suffering flooding due to deforestation and must be among the 23 countries whose food production is falling. Bangladesh shares with the Netherlands, London and the Fens a fear of the rising sea level caused by the greenhouse effect; 85% of its area lies within 100 feet of sea level so much of it would cease to exist.

Might not churches in the Fens therefore profitably *covenant* with their counterparts in Bangladesh to work for a reduction in greenhouse gases and to plan for the effects of drought and a rise in sea level if this cannot be achieved? Missionary societies could assist in identifying churches in Bangladesh, and Christian Aid and Tear Fund might facilitate the exchange of personnel.

Cambridge schoolchildren might 'twin' with their counterparts in, say, Rotterdam, in order to study strategies for keeping the sea at bay (which would have a salutary effect on adult awareness of the problem), and estimates could be made of the main causes of carbon dioxide production and ways of reducing it.

Churches in Bangladesh, Rotterdam and Cambridge could provide convenient vantage points for exploring some of the concerns about trade expressed in chapter five (possibly in coordination with Traidcraft). The presence of a predominantly Bangladeshi mosque in Cambridge would increase awareness of the culture and social and economic history of

Bangladesh and might lead to some interesting inter-faith conversations. The Church Urban Fund could be used to make contact with Bangladeshi communities in London and Manchester, where problems of racism are rampant. Thus an environmental point of entry into JPIC could lead to concern about justice . . . and perhaps peace as well.

The suggestion of the Basle report that peace education be introduced at all levels, including schools, might not achieve a consensus among churches in Kent (though the Scots, with their vast array of NATO armaments, might think otherwise!). But Kent schoolchildren might be encouraged to explore the safety of personnel working in the Channel tunnel, and to press, together with their counterparts at the other end in France, for the monitoring and control of car exhaust fumes.

To try to state what additional covenants there ought to be is contrary to JPIC's participative bottom-up style, but there are several areas in which a JPIC connection might enhance causes which may have been conceived too narrowly. Thus, for example, the need for racial integration in Britain might profitably be argued more from the point of view of the positive value of ethnic pluralism than in terms of the narrower appeal for justice.

Homosexuality might also benefit from discussion within a broader context. The Vancouver Assembly mandated the WCC to undertake a study of homosexuality in relation to human rights. But in spite of lobbying by the Dutch churches this has not been done, largely on account of resistance by other constituencies.

This is disappointing, especially because many churches look to the WCC to give a lead on controversial issues, as it did in the late seventies with the programme to combat racism. It is interesting to note that black South Africans, including Allan Boesak, have expressed concern at the harassment of homosexuals and lesbians in Europe, and are much more willing to see the issue as a violation of human rights than members of some other African churches (e.g. at the last Lambeth Conference). It remains to be seen whether or not United Europe will mean a better deal for lesbians and gay men, and whether or not Britain's invidious Clause 28 will survive the Single European Act for long.

Events in Eastern Europe are too recent to be evaluated, but it is to be hoped that the covenanting process among churches here will take cognisance of them. Christians in the former German Democratic Republic were relating their commitment to justice and peace to the state of their environment even before the Vancouver Assembly, and some of their leading thinkers have played a major role in the WCC's JPIC programme. The Kirchentag Movement of young, radical Germans has already devoted considerable attention to JPIC at its biennial meetings, and will be a major resource for the churches and for society as they move towards United Europe.

How will British churches fare in relation to their Continental counterparts? In many ways British churchgoing has more in common with the rest of Europe than with, say, the USA, where people are more inclined to express their faith via attendance at church. But British religious institutions are very different from those on the Continent, and the Church of England, with its characteristic Englishness and membership of the Anglican Communion – a framework in which the European contribution is minimal – is likely to experience greater difficulty in creating a European consciousness in Britain than, say, Roman Catholics and Presbyterians (especially in Scotland), who already have strong European links. But despite the growing assimilation of Roman Catholics into English society, it remains to be seen how non-church going Anglicans will react to increased contact with the Roman Catholic Church, and whether or not minorities on both sides of the Channel will join forces (e.g. English Catholics and French Protestants).

It is to be hoped that the European churches will follow up the recommendations of the Basle Assembly as summarised in the last chapter, and in particular will facilitate the widest possible discussion of the *Brundtland Report,* with its clear ethical mandate to meet our present needs without compromising the ability of future generations to do the same. The British churches might well encourage detailed analysis of the Report via the recently constituted churches energy group chaired by Sir Frank Layfield. Reference has been made to the feasibility of dealing with climatic problems in conjunction with ongoing discussions of energy problems. The UN Earth Summit will also require careful evaluation and the implementation of its proposals. (See Appendix for the statement on this by the Environmental Issues Network and resolution by the February 1992 CCBI Assembly.)

It remains to be seen what kind of ethical framework is adopted by European nations and churches in the next decade. It has already been suggested that most European nations are effectively secular in their approaches to ethical problems, but some churches may well want their governments to adopt more explicitly Christian positions. Perhaps the most realistic way forward for the churches is to find as much common ground as possible with secular points of view, and to make specific contributions on particular issues on which they are recognised as having competence and a legitimate interest – the beginning and end of life, for example. We have seen in earlier chapters some interesting ethical theories and points of view which could assist the churches in making such contributions. Thus, for example, Göran Collste's secular ethic based on the maximum gratification of basic human needs might help to keep the concerns of the developing world and of future generations in view, theocentric ethics could achieve much the same for the environment, Archbishop Kirill's appeal for common moral principles could find echoes in the minds of European decision-makers, and James Gustafson's distinctions between prophetic, narrative, ethical and policy types of moral discourse could help everybody to say what they want to say more cogently and persuasively.

Little has been said about worship, but there is a major task for the churches to express liturgically just about all of what has been said in these chapters. Reference has been made to connections between worship and work, and the use of the offertory to express 'the fruit of our labours, the work of our hands'. But the liturgical affirmation of the totality of all creation could have a revolutionary effect on conventional worship in terms of its content (e.g. hymns and prayers affirming nature), a greater level of participation on the part of groups who have traditionally been excluded (e.g. women and children), and a challenge to people's lifestyles. How might some church members feel, for example, if prior to receiving communion the prayer of confession invited them to consider the efficiency and environmental compatibility of their mode of transport to church?

One hopes that United Europe will see increased collaboration between the Roman Catholic Church and other European churches. A major strength of the Basle Assembly and much of the work summarised earlier has been the full participation of the Roman Catholic Church.

As Britain's new and exciting ecumenical partnership between the Roman Catholic and other British churches gets under way, may we not hope that the WCC will covenant to enter into a similar process of negotiations leading to full and equal partnership with Rome?

Appendix

COUNCIL OF CHURCHES FOR BRITAIN AND IRELAND

ENVIRONMENT AND DEVELOPMENT

The Council of Churches for Britain and Ireland, via its Environmental Issues Network

i) welcomes the United Nations initiative in setting up the Commission on Environment and Development (UNCED), chaired by Mrs Gro Harlem Brundtland;

ii) looks forward to the forthcoming summit in Rio de Janeiro in June 1992 and urges the fullest participation by British and Irish Government representatives.

The Network calls on the churches to assert that 'sustainable development' (i.e. development that meets the needs of the present without compromising the ability of future generations to meet their own needs) is a goal which expresses the Christian imperative to love and serve God the Creator and to love our neighbours, many of whom are children predominantly in the southern continents.

The Network also calls on the churches to recognise the importance of the six major components of the UNCED process, summarised as follows:

a) An Earth Charter, described officially as 'a declaration of basic principles for the conduct of Nations and peoples in respect of environment and development to ensure the future viability and integrity of the Earth as a hospitable home for human and other forms of life'.

b) International agreements of specific legal measures on global climate change, forests and biodiversity.

c) Agenda 21 – assigning international action, priorities, costs and responsibilities during the next century in relation to specific environmental aspects of agriculture, forests, the atmosphere and the need for clean drinkable water and to economic questions including world debts and aid flows.

d) North-South technology transfer.

e) The provision of new or additional financial resources.

f) The strengthening of the institutional capacities and processes which will implement or monitor all agreements.

In responding, the churches in Britain and Ireland are especially concerned to see that the developmental issues of the South addressed

103

and that adequate resources be allocated to meet them. Much of the pollution and resource depletion experienced throughout the world is the result of activities by industrial countries which have increased their assets and improved their lifestyles while concealing or ignoring the true cost of environmental damage. Industrial countries must shoulder the economic cost of addressing the environmental and developmental problems to which they have so heavily contributed.

Similarly the churches, prompted by their overseas aid and mission agencies, and in keeping with the biblical principle of Jubilee, urge that commercial and government debts incurred by the poorer nations during recent decades be cancelled or rescheduled possibly in return for environmental guarantees within the scope of international agreements referred to in b) above. It is intolerable that there should continue to be a net transfer from the impoverished developing nations to the industrial nations.

In their commitment to these developmental and environmental concerns the churches reaffirm the scriptural emphasis on justice which has been a guiding principle in the traditions of the churches. That emphasis was clearly expressed through the European Ecumenical Assembly in Basle in 1989 when the churches of Europe committed themselves to seek peace with justice for the whole creation.

The Assembly of the Council of Churches for Britain and Ireland calls on the churches throughout these islands to pray for all who will take part in the UNCED meeting in Rio de Janeiro in June and offers prayerful support to Rachel Stephens and David Gosling who will be attending on their behalf.

Select Bibliography

Angel, David J. R., Comer, J. D. and Wilkinson, M. L. N., *Sustaining Earth*, Macmillan, 1990.

Birch, L. Charles, *On Purpose*, New South Wales University Press Ltd., 1990.

Cardosa, Ernesto and Gianelli, Marcos, *'And God saw that it was good . . .'*, WCC, Geneva, 1989.

Carino, Feliciano and Gosling, David, eds., *Technology from the Underside*, NCCP, Manila, 1986.

Davis, Howard and Gosling, David, eds., *Will the Future Work?*, WCC, Geneva, 1986.

Duchrow, Ulrich and Liedke, Gerhard, *Shalom*, WCC, Geneva, 1989.

Edwards, David L., *Christians in a New Europe*, Collins (Fount Paperbacks), 1990.

Engel, J. R. and J. G., eds., *Ethics of Environment and Development*, Belhaven Press, 1990.

Gosling, David and Musschenga, Bert, eds., *Science Education and Ethical Values*, WCC, Geneva, and Georgetown University Press, Washington, D. C., 1985.

Gustafson, James N., *Ethics from a Theocentric Perspective*, Vol. 2, University of Chicago Press, 1984.

Küng, Hans, *Global Responsibility*, SCM, 1991.

Limouris, Gennadios, *Justice, Peace and the Integrity of Creation: Insights from Orthodoxy*, WCC, Geneva, 1990.

McFague, Sallie, *Models of God*, Fortress Press, Philadelphia, 1987.

Merchant, Caroline, *The Death of Nature*, Harper and Row, San Francisco, 1987.

Moltmann, Jürgen, *God in Creation*, SCM Press, 1985.

Montefiore, Hugh and Gosling, David, eds., *Nuclear Crisis: A Question of Breeding*, Prism Press, 1977.

Newbigin, Lesslie, *The Other Side of 1984*, BCC, 1983/WCC, 1984.

Newbigin, Lesslie, *Foolishness to the Greeks*, SPCK, 1986.

Niles, D. Preman, *Resisting the Threats to Life*, WCC, Geneva, 1989.

Polkinghorne, John, *Science and Providence: God's Interaction with the World*, SPCK, 1989.

Pullinger, David J., ed., *With Scorching Heat and Drought?*, SRT Project, Edinburgh, 1989.

Reardon, John, ed., *Threads of a Creation: A Resource Book of Words and Pictures*, United Reformed Church, 1989.

North-South: A Programme for Survival, Brandt Report, Pan Books, 1980.
Shaping Tomorrow, Home Mission Division of the Methodist Church, 1981.
Future Conditional, Home Mission Division of the Methodist Church, 1983.
Celebrating One World: A Resource Book on Liturgy and Social Justice, CAFOD and Thomas More Centre, 1987.
Our Common Future, Oxford University Press, 1987.
The Truth Shall Make You Free, Report of the 1988 Lambeth Conference, Church House Publishing, London, 1988.
Banking on the Poor, Christian Aid, 1988.
Peace with Justice, Conference of European Churches, Geneva, 1989.
While Earth Endures . . ., Centre for JPIC, Scottish Churches Council, Dunblane, 1989.
First Things First, BCC and Christian Aid, 1989.
The Forgotten Trinity, 1 Report of the BCC Study Commission on Trinitarian Doctrine Today, BCC, 1989; 2 Study Guide on issues contained in the Report, BCC, 1989; 3 A Selection of Papers presented to the BCC Study Commission, BCC/CCBI, 1991.

Church and Society Documents, WCC, Geneva, as follows:
(1) *AIDS and the Church*, March 1987.
(2) *God, Humanity and Nature in Relation to Justice and Peace*, September 1987.
(3) *Reintegrating God's Creation*, September 1987.
(4) *Science and the Theology of Creation*, August 1988.
(5) *Creation and the Kingdom of God*, August 1988.
(6) *Caring for Creation*, August 1988 (also in Spanish).
(7) *Workbook on Afforestation*, June 1989 (Spanish only).
(8) *Your Health is in Your Hands*, October 1988.
(9) *People for Forests*, April 1989.

Report and Background Papers of Working Committee on Church and Society, WCC, Geneva, as follows:
(1) Potsdam, formerly GDR, July 1986.
(2) Glion, Switzerland, September 1987.
(3) Tambov, formerly USSR, September 1988.

Index of Names

Addy, Tony 88
Ahmed, Akbar. 93
Alexi, Patriarch 74
Alfonsin, Raoul 13
Ariyaratne, A. T. 26
Arnold, John 74

Baldwin, James. 76
Barth, Karl 59
Bartholomew, Courtney 44
Beijiko, Roma 35
Bena-Silu 45
Benn, Tony 5
Bernard, R. P. 46, 47
Birch, Charles 57, 58, 59,
   61, 66, 67, 94, 95
Bleakley, David 80
Boesak, Allan. 24, 100
Bohm, David 57
Bonhoeffer, Dietrich 86
Brandt, Willy. 3
Browning, Bishop Edmund . . 37, 45
de Brum, Tony. 31
Bruntland, Gro Harlem. 21, 81, 103
Burns, Robert. 87

Carson, Rachel 2
Carter, President Jimmy 21
Castro, Emilio 37, 42
Clare, Mother Mary 92
Cobb, John B. 50, 51, 59, 95
Collste, Göran 55, 56, 86, 101
Cowap, Chris. 7, 21
Crocker, John 96

Darwin, Charles. 2

Ecumenical Patriarch. 89
Elliot, Alison 87
Elliott, Charles. 64

Falcke, Heino. 67
Feofan, Bishop 41, 61
Francis, Saint. 42
Furlong, Monica 87

Gandhi, Indira. 11
Gandhi, M. K.. 26
Gibson, William E.. 28
Gill, Robin. 65
Gordon, Kevin. 44, 45, 47
Gustafson, James 69, 70,
   96, 98, 102

Habgood, Archbishop John 45
Hardy, Sir Alister 25, 49
Harrison, Paul 12
Hoiore-Atger, Céline 37
Hypher, Paul 13

John Paul II, Pope. 54, 89

Kant, Immanuel. 1, 2
Kapita, Biel 44
Karim, Wazir-Jahan. 17
Keju-Johnson, Darlene 31, 32,
   33, 35, 70
Keju-Johnson, Giff 31
Kerr, Charles 31
Kim, Yong Bock 27
Kirill, Archbishop 40,88ff., 102
Kohl, Helmut. 3

Laeyendecker-Thung, Mady 65
Lau, Bernard 31
Layfield, Sir Frank. 101
Leuenberger, Theodor. 53

McDaniel, Jay 61
McFague, Sallie 29
McManus, James 44

Mandela, Nelson 11
Mann, Jonathan. 45
Martini, Cardinal 74
Maximus, Saint 61
Maxwell, Stephen 79
May, John 90
Mbiti, John 24
Mercado, Bishop La Verne. 16
Midgley, Mary 26
Mugambi, Jesse 24, 49
Myers, Norman 16

Nemenzo, Fidel 16
Newbigin, Lesslie. 64, 95
Newton, Isaac 57

Oommen, T. K. 65

Pannenberg, Wolfhart. 59, 65
Parker, Lord Justice 5
Peacocke, Arthur. 65
Penttila, Pirkko 40
Philaret, Metropolitan. 41
Philip, Prince 46
Plunkett, Michael 88
Pobee, John S. 23
Polkinghorne, John 58, 59,
    61, 65, 67, 95
Porritt, Jonathon 81

Riegner, Gerhardt 41
Robinson, Bishop John 25, 49
Runcie, Lord Robert 73, 91

Scott, Sir Walter 81
Seller, Mary 62
Senturias, Erlinda 31
Seremane, Joe 24
Setiloane, Gabriel 25, 26, 49
Sin, Jaime Cardinal. 16, 19,
    53, 54, 95
Smart, Michael 80
Sowunmi, Adebisi 23
de Sweemer, Cécile. 38

Tabibi, Abdul H. 42
Thatcher, Margaret 21, 81
Tracy, David 70, 96
Trudeau, Pierre 11
Tull, Tom. 44

Viravaidya, Mechai 46

Ward, Barbara 73
Ward, Keith 59
Whitehead, A. N. 51, 57, 59
Wilardjo, Liek 18
Wynne, Brian 40

Yates, Bishop John 73